Also by James Castagno

Octavia and the Greek Key

The Lady of the Lantern

Dance of the Red Panel

Witness to Terror
Fugitive Series Book One

Out of Tunis
Fugitive Series Book Two

Out of Naples
Fugitive Series Book Three

The Fugitive Series
Three International Crime Novellas

Come Nemesis

James Castagno

JUDAS IN THE MIDST

**The Witness Security Program had seen nothing like it.
Then the ballerina arrived.**

James Castagno

A Novella

JUDAS IN THE MIDST is a work of fiction. No classified or confidential information was accessed or used in composing this manuscript. All details are a compilation of open source documentation, or publicly released information. All characters, businesses, places, events or incidents either are the products of the author's imagination or are used fictitiously. Any resemblance to actual persons, living or dead, or actual events and locales is purely coincidental.

Cover Design: James Castagno.
La Ballerina: Insegnante di danza classica, Flora Vitolo, Salerno, Italia.

I have learned to hate all traitors, and there is no disease that I spit on more than treachery.

– *Aeschylus*

James Castagno

CHAPTER I

A NEW CASE

Paul Baldini reached to the bedside table and turned off the cell phone alarm. He got out of bed, walked to the dresser, and stared at a framed photo of him and his wife. They stood on a balcony outside a restaurant on the island of Santorini, Greece. She wore a light teal summer dress with leather sandals trimmed to match. In the background were pure white buildings and a single blue dome topped with a crucifix. Below a cruise ship lay anchored in the azure water of the southern Aegean Sea.

He lifted a worn piece of paper and read his wife's note. "I hate being away from you. When I return, let's go to dinner at the beach. Love, Celeste."

Paul set the note back beside the picture. His eyes caught his Rolex GMT Master on the opposite side of the frame. He stared at it a moment, picked it up, and turned it. On the back-cover was the inscription *I Love You, Celeste.*

###

Two hours later Paul had changed into pressed jeans, and an untucked and unbuttoned gray short-sleeve shirt over a black T-shirt. The white image of an eagle on the T-shirt peered ahead. He and a uniformed police officer exited the monorail from the main terminal of Tampa International Airport. They stopped and shook hands.

"Thanks for the company," Paul said. "You better get back to work. Tell the wife and kids I said hello."

"I will. How long you going to be here?"

Paul hated to lie. "Not long if my friend's plane is on time. No more than an hour."

"Have a good day." The officer started toward the boarding side for the monorail for his ride back to the main terminal.

Paul removed the airport badge from around his neck and shoved it into his pocket. It was good to talk with an old friend, but an armed officer would draw unnecessary attention at gate 31 on Airside C. He walked to the gate where a Southwest Airlines flight was scheduled to arrive in five minutes.

At Gate 31, he reached into the pocket, removed a folded piece of paper, and stared at it. "Tatiana Demko. Five-foot-nine. Twenty-six-year-old ballet dancer." He ripped the paper into small pieces and threw it into a trash can.

The thought of running into someone that recognized him crossed his mind. It had happened before and coming up with a good lie was a pain in the ass. He was going to meet a young lady, walk with her to baggage claim, and leave the airport with her in his SUV. *I can hear it now. Baldini's got a girlfriend. Wonder where he found her?* He'd have to think of a story to tell if that happened.

Paul removed his phone from his back pocket, tapped the screen, and waited for an answer. He reached under the left side of his open shirt and shoved the shoulder holster farther back. Should his Glock 45 Auto be seen, it would not only raise eyebrows, it may cause a stampede from the gate.

A faint hello came through the phone speaker.

"Hi Mark, how's the witness security business in Musicland, USA?"

Mark Hale, an Inspector U.S. Marshal colleague chuckled. "Parts of Nashville never change. The same old shit-kicking bands on Broadway. As for work, they've got me loaded with six cases. You calling about WC-9269?"

"Yeah. Damn, it just hit me." Paul cocked his head to the side. "How long has WITSEC been using four digit Witness Control numbers?"

"I think since the beginning. I once looked at a list and WC-0005 was on it."

"Soon we'll be above ten thousand. Anyway, I read part of this girl's file. Her boyfriend and his friends are part of a large international Russian crime syndicate. When's he getting out of the joint?"

"The way he's putting Russian mobsters in jail, I don't think they'll keep him longer than four more years."

"I took a look at her picture ... she's pretty. Need to pick her out in the crowd. What's she wearing?"

"Remember the broad we picked up last year in the Miami airport?"

Paul paused a moment and grinned. "Yeah, the one with the see-through shirt, and no bra. I'll never forget the red miniskirt and screaming snot-nosed three-year-old clinging to her pinky finger. Wonder what the people staring at us thought?"

"If the kid wasn't there, we would have looked like two guys arranging an afternoon threesome. The young lady I'm sending you is not that type. She has a good head on her shoulders. It won't be difficult to spot her. I walked her to the gate this morning. When I put her on the plane, she had on tight black pants and a black bra."

"Great. She's flying half naked?"

"No, you'll see. I told her to stay near the gate and wait for you to approach. She won't recognize you, but I gave her your first name. She has her new name documentation ... should be an easy case."

"Psychopaths looking for an advantage. None of them are easy to handle."

"It's the quick and the dead, Paul. We both need to strive to stay the former."

"You're right."

"Listen. She's not one of our normal witnesses. You'll understand once you read through the file I sent and spend time with her. One thing though, she has two small problems you need know."

Paul shook his head and rolled his eyes. *I always get the nut jobs.* "What?"

"She attracts men like kids to ice cream covered with jimmies. The other one I can't talk about."

"Nice. I'm supposed to wallow around in the swamp and wait for the alligators?"

"I wouldn't do that to you. You'll get a call from the Deputy Chief of WITSEC. I wish I could say more. You'll know why I can't when you talk to him. Be careful."

Paul's phone beeped, and he tapped the screen.

"Damn, your Houdini moment. Just got a message to call him today at two."

"On the secure phone?"

"Yeah."

"Good. He'll fill you in with the details. Also, in the file there's a report about her being a dual U.S. and Ukrainian citizen. Text me when you have her in tow."

"Will do."

"Oh, by the way. She's excited she's going to Florida. While I had her, she took a two day trip to Disney World. She loved it. If something else comes to mind, I'll call you."

"Okay, take care, Mark." He ended the call and took a second look at the message from his old friend, John Colombus. *Don't get calls from someone at the top often. It's got to be important.* He walked to a chair in front of and facing away from the gate desk. Seated in front of a smoked glass panel, he focused on a clear reflection of the exit from the passenger boarding bridge.

The flight was announced and as the passengers entered the gate area, he looked at each of them. Thirty people passed before he saw the black bra. He now understood why Mark mentioned it. It stood out from under the sheer cream sleeveless tunic.

She walked past him with perfect posture, and her head up, as she pulled a hard-case red aluminum carry-on. *That thing set her back a few hundred bucks.* Her long hair was pulled back, tied with a black ribbon and hung over her shoulder.

He let her step to the center of the walkway, stop, and survey those around her. With the grace of a ballerina she turned in a circle, checking out everyone near the gate.

Nice clothes, a dancer's body, and carries herself well. Easy to tell why men take an interest. He got out of his chair and approached her from behind.

"Dobroho ranku, Tatiana."

She froze and eased her head around. Wide eyes glanced over her shoulder.

Paul tapped his chest. "I'm Paul."

The look of uncertainty on her face subsided. "You scared me ... you speak Ukrainian?"

"No. Good morning is the only phrase I know." He hesitated and looked into her eyes. "In the few words you spoke, you didn't have an accent."

"I was born in New York City but never lived in America. My father was the director of a Ukrainian dance company. My mother gave birth while he was producing a show on Broadway."

"Then English is your second language."

"Yes. A couple of girls I danced with were American. For over two years they helped me with my American English. Besides Ukrainian, I speak Russian, French, German, and Italian. If a ballerina wants to work in Europe, she must be able to communicate."

Paul smiled. *This one is a smart cookie.* "I'm stuck on English and a little Italian ... mostly cuss words." He motioned down the concourse, and they started toward baggage claim.

"How was your flight?"

"Good, but someone was trying to get a little more than friendly. The young man sitting next to me asked if I wanted to go to dinner while I was in Tampa."

Paul smiled. *She's beautiful. Why wouldn't he? Drop it.*

"How many more bags do you have?"

"Two." She pulled her carry-on to her side. "Both are a little larger than this."

"We'll get your luggage and drive to Clearwater Beach. I rented a suite overlooking the pool at a place called Coconut Cove. I'm sure you'll enjoy it there."

On their way to baggage claim, many lingering glances turned in their direction. No one, not even the ladies, checked him out.

Later that day after settling Tatiana in the suite, Paul turned the corner and walked to his office door in the building on West Kennedy Boulevard in Tampa. He glanced at the eye-level sign on the wall next to the entrance. It read, Paul Baldini, OEO. DOJ. Any sign identifying the office as WITSEC Tampa Metro was out of the question.

He unlocked the dead bolt, entered a six-digit code into the keypad next to the door handle, and walked into a five-by-five-foot space. The steel door in front of him held its own keypad that unlocked the door and turned off the alarm system.

Once through the door, he crossed a waiting room furnished with two chairs and a coffee table. On his way to his office at the end of the hall, he passed two more steel doors with keypads.

Paul wasn't the type person to flaunt what he had, or complain about what he didn't have. His office wasn't over the top. Two padded chairs sat in front of his executive desk. Against the wall behind them, stood a coffee table in front of a brown leather loveseat. The walls held several large photos of Clearwater Beach. Nothing in the room identified him as an Inspector, Witness Security Specialist.

He removed the shirt concealing his weapon, took off his shoulder holster, and placed both over hooks on the coat tree next to the door. As he dropped into the chair behind his desk, he glanced at his watch and reached for a legal pad and pen. He lifted the handset of his *Sectéra vIPer* Secure Phone and dialed.

He recognized John Colombus' voice when he said, "Hello."

"Hi, Chief. You asked me to call at two."

"Thank you, Paul. Let's go secure before we start."

Paul pressed the SECURE button on the phone and stared at the blue light below it. The light continued to blink for ten seconds and then become solid. The computerized voice announced, "Line is secure."

"Everything okay on your end?" Paul asked.

"Yes. Did you get our Ms. Ukraine settled?"

"I did. I'll meet her again tomorrow."

"I spoke with Mark Hale this morning. I'm the one who decided to send you the case. You need to be cautious."

"That's what Mark implied. What's going on, John?"

"The information is a little old but still valid. A month ago, NSA intercepted a call about her and her boyfriend. It was a short conversation. Important people in Russia are concerned the boyfriend will give them up. No one thinks much of it, but I'm troubled. The call originated in the Kremlin. It was to someone in the Russian embassy in Washington."

Paul bit his bottom lip and stared across the room. "How much do they know about her situation?"

"They're sure she's in the program, but nothing else. I've clamped down on access to her file. Here at headquarters, your Branch Chief, Case Analyst, and I, are the only people that can get information on her. She doesn't show up as an active case in Tampa."

Paul shook his head. "What about the Case Manager?"

"We're picking someone this evening. That desk has been empty for too long. I'm not going to add the new guy to the list yet. I'll let him get settled before I tell him she's with you."

"It's that bad?"

"Yes. Mark and your Chief in Miami are the only two in the field who know you have her in Tampa. Her original file is still accessible to everyone, but it ends with her termination a few weeks ago. She has a new limited access file in our computer system. As for NSA's report, Bob Plummer has a copy of it in his vault in Miami."

"Any need-to-know problems with me getting access to it?"

"No. Go over to Miami and tell him you want to read it. It's good to have a one-on-one with your boss in case you need to call in the cavalry."

"I'll talk to him later today."

The phone fell silent, and a moment passed. Paul furrowed his brow. "You still there, John?"

"Yeah, sorry. I had to locate my notes about our next witness, WC-6121."

"My Iranian. No problems I hope, he's doing well."

"No. Remember the request you had us send to the CIA?"

"Which one?"

"His father's health."

Paul shook his head. "Yeah. They can't knock on his door in Tehran and ask him how he's doing, but it's been nine months."

"I guess assets in the Islamic Republic are few and far between. They finally have answers, and two of their people want to meet with him."

"When?"

"The middle of next week. Send him up to Nashville. Mark will handle it from there. As soon as Mark calls me, I'll tell the guys at the Agency what time we'll get him to Langley."

"Tell Mark to send me his return itinerary. I'll pick him up at the airport."

"I will. Now back to the beautiful Tatiana. I'll press NSA to find out if they have any more information. Let's pray they're not tight lipped. I'll pass what I get to you. Watch your ass."

"Thanks, Chief. It's best if I head to Miami tomorrow and meet her when I get back. Can't tell her much, but she needs to be security conscious."

"Okay, Paul. Call me if you need help."

The phone went dead and Paul set the handset into its cradle. He lifted his cell phone from his desk and dialed.

"Hello."

"Tatiana, its Paul." He waited for a response. "Are you—"

"Is something wrong?"

"No, I'm going to Miami tomorrow. I won't be able to come as planned."

"Everything is fine. I'll keep busy going to the pool, and the beach. Call to tell me when you are coming so I'll be here."

CHAPTER II

THE SITE

Paul walked out of the American Airlines baggage claim door at Miami International Airport and jumped into the Lincoln Navigator waiting at the curb. He nodded to his boss, Chief Inspector Bob Plummer.

Bob put the SUV into gear. "Damn, glad you came early ... we'll beat the traffic. How was the flight?"

Paul looked at him and pressed his lips together.

Bob pulled into passing traffic. "Why did I ask that dumb question? Sorry."

"No sweat. It's my problem, not yours."

"Maria will be the only one in the office. Got a small protection detail in Ft. Lauderdale."

"You have someone at a District Court trial?"

"A pilot. He'll be on the witness stand for three days. Caught him coming from the Bahamas with a load of pot. DEA put the squeeze on him, and he turned on four traffickers."

"Big time?"

"No, locals out of the Berry Islands. They were using a private airstrip."

"Is he a prisoner witness?"

"Not yet. Won't be sentenced until after he finishes testifying. There's another case that will be heard here in Miami."

When they reached downtown, Bob pulled into the underground parking garage and into a reserved space.

They walked to the WITSEC Metro office.

Maria was waiting for them when they came through the second door into the office space. She hugged Paul. "What brings you to the big city?"

"I need to rummage around in your files. How are you and the family?"

"The old man works too much. Kids just started college."

Paul grinned. "Two of them at the same time will keep you both working for a few more years."

Bob started across the room. "Come on, I'll get the file."

They entered a control room housing a panel of surveillance monitors and a wall lined with five drawer security cabinets. On slow days no one paid attention to the screens unless a camera motion sensor alarm sounded.

Bob walked into the open vault and he remained near the door as Bob stopped in front of a five drawer security cabinet. He spun the combination lock, opened the drawer, and removed a folder with an orange Top Secret cover sheet attached. "We'll go to the conference room where you can read it."

Paul sat at the table reading the report. "Have you read this?"

"Yeah. It's amazing the information they can get."

He raised the report. "Has anyone tried to find out who in the Russian Embassy is going to work this?"

"Not yet." Bob grinned. "You can bet your ass the GRU has quite a few people running around the United States."

"GRU?"

"Main Intelligence Directorate of the Russian army. Don't let the word army fool you. They're like stink on shit ... everywhere. They'll work with other Russian assets. I'll call John later. Maybe we'll get lucky and he'll have the latest information."

Paul slid the report across the table. "Without something to go on, there's not much I can do."

"Stay proactive." His boss picked up the folder. "Keep your eyes open." He grinned. "If you see a Russian ... run."

"Great, I'll look for sweat pouring out from under the fucking fur hats. It's my ass that's hanging out there. I'll be plugged into my surroundings."

"Come on. Let's go for a late breakfast ... early lunch. When we get back, we'll rattle the Deputy Chief's cage."

"After we speak to him I need to head to the airport. I'm meeting the new girl in the morning."

CHAPTER III

CAUTION

The next day Paul drove to Clearwater Beach. He knocked on the door to the second floor unit overlooking the pool and glanced at his watch. *Ten minutes early.*

Prior to leaving Miami, he and Bob spoke with John Colombus. He had asked John to light a fire under a few asses to see if any other information was available. Information from NSA didn't come easy. If anyone could talk them into helping WITSEC, it was John. In the meantime he'd tell Tatiana to keep her eyes and ears open.

He turned when his name was called.

Tatiana approached wearing a red bikini and holding a towel. She smiled. "It's not ten yet, you're early."

"I wasn't sure how much traffic there'd be coming across the bridge."

She unlocked the door and stepped into the unit.

Paul's eyes lowered to the back of the thong. *Not much that doesn't get tanned.* He shook his head. *Better watch my ass and not hers.*

She spoke without looking back at him. "Come in. I'll be back in a minute. I want to get out of this wet bathing suit." She untied the top before entering the bedroom and then closed the door.

Paul took a seat in a chair across from the couch.

Tatiana stepped out of the bedroom in a pair of tight leggings and a blue tube top. She lowered herself onto the couch, raised both legs and crossed them. "How was Miami?"

"Crowded."

"Was my name mentioned?"

"A couple of times. We want to make sure you're safe. Have you met anyone yet?"

"No."

"Good. Let's discuss what you're going to tell people."

"I know what I'm going to say." She got up and adjusted her top. "You want something to drink?" She strolled to the small kitchen.

Those pants are a second skin. He turned away. "A glass of water will do."

She returned with two waters and gracefully lowered herself to the couch. "Mark explained everything to me when I was in Nashville. I performed a few times in New York City with the troupe out of London. I'm going to say I lived there. I'm familiar with the city ... people won't be suspicious."

Have to remember this case isn't new. "Good. In a couple of days we'll start looking for an apartment to rent. In a day or so, I'll bring you a map and a couple of magazines about this area. You can pick where you might want to live. I'll let you know if it's a good choice."

"I want to stay near the beach."

"It's expensive on this side of the bridge, we'll see. Mark most likely told you things to avoid."

"He did."

"There's one other thing I want to mention. Many foreigners visit this part of Florida ... even from Eastern Europe and Russia. If you hear anyone speaking an East Slavic language or Russian, I want you get away from them and call me at once."

"Is there something you're not telling me?"

"No. I'm security conscious ... you're important to me."

She smiled and placed a hand over her heart. "No one has said that to me in a long time."

Paul grinned to hide the alarming butterflies in his gut. *Jesus, next time pick better words.* Time spent working a female witness, who happened to be a knockout, without the support of a female inspector, could become job threatening. "All my cases are important. You've placed your life in my hands." *Shut up! You're digging the hole deeper.*

She stared at him and took a sip of water. "You're married?" She pointed at his wedding band. "The ring."

Paul twisted the ring around his finger. He had no intention to start a conversation about his personal life. "I was. My wife is deceased."

She stiffened and a shocked expression appeared. "I'm sorry. What happened?"

"Let's just say she died." He stood. "Relax for a few days. I have things I need to do today. I'll come to see you on Tuesday at one. We'll discuss areas you might want to live. Somewhere not far from the beach."

Tatiana walked him to the door. "Thank you. I'll be here Tuesday when you arrive."

After he returned to his office, Paul sat at his desk reading Mark's reports about Tatiana. He closed the file as his cell phone beeped.

A tap on the screen opened a new text message. Paul stared at it.

Merit Promotion Announcement: Inspector Victor Serban, Pittsburgh Metro, has been chosen as the new Southeast Case Manager.

"Where the hell did he come from ... never heard of him." He closed the message, grabbed the handset to his secure telephone, hit the speaker button, and called Mark.

He answered after the first ring. "Hi, Paul."

"Did you get the message announcing the new Case Manager?"

"Yeah."

"You know him?"

"By name ... never met him."

"Me neither. How long has he been with WITSEC?"

"I talked to the Anjoli a few minutes ago ... she knows him. Said he transferred over from the Court Security Division a little over a year ago. His family is from the D.C. ... wanted to get close to home."

Paul furrowed his brow. "Did she say anything else?"

"Said his grandfather was a wealthy business owner when Moldova was controlled by the Soviets."

Paul tilted his head and for a moment stared at his desk. "That was a few years back."

"Yeah. Before the fall of the Iron Curtain. Still has family there. Give her a call."

"I will. Been shooting lately?"

"Keeping my regular schedule. At least three times a week. You?"

"The same. The guys at the gun shop said they're going to name a lane on their range after me. Let me go so I can call Anjoli."

"Okay. Buzz me if you need my help."

Paul hung up, dialed another number and waited for the familiar voice to answer.

"Yes."

He grinned. "Good. I'm glad you agree with me ... it won't cost much."

Anjoli wasted no time replying. "Paul, I answer the phone that way. I agree to nothing."

He chuckled. "How's life in the puzzle palace?"

"Good, I'm glad you called. When we discuss your new case don't refer to a name or WC number. Just refer to the new one."

"Will do. Wanted to ask you about the guy who was picked as the new Case Manager. Ever met him?"

"A few times. He's nice."

"What can you tell me about him?" Paul picked up a pen and slid a legal pad to his side.

"He was born in D.C. and graduated from Georgetown."

"Well, he must be smart. Think he can handle the job?"

"He's only been in WITSEC for a year ... a little green, but I'll keep him out of trouble. I'm on my way to see the Branch Chief, you need anything else?"

"No. Once the new one settles in, I'll call. Take care."

"It's going to be difficult keeping that case from everyone else. Contact me if there's something I can do."

"Thanks, Anjoli." Paul replaced the handset in the phone, stood, and headed to the door.

CHAPTER IV

SANTINO AND THE COFFEE GUY

The next morning, Paul drove south from downtown Clearwater to Belleair. He pulled into the driveway of a white, two-story home on Flamingo Drive.

He rang the bell and Santino Genetti opened the door. "Come in."

Five-foot-eight Santino, was a well-built man of sixty-five. His full head of gray hair, combed straight back, was never out of place.

Paul stepped into the house and glanced at Genetti's clothes. "Black dress pants, a white silk shirt, and loafers. Jesus, Tino. Do you ever wear jeans and a T-shirt?"

"No. Always dress nice. People show you more respect." Tino waved a hand at him. "You always wear two shirts, one unbuttoned and not tucked into your pants?"

Paul pulled back the left side of his shirt exposing the Glock 45 in a black leather shoulder holster. He grinned. "In case I need the tools of my trade."

Santino laughed and shoved him toward the kitchen.

Tino's petite, gray-haired wife, standing near the espresso machine, greeted Paul with a smile.

"Good morning, coffee?"

"Yes, thank you, Pina."

The large kitchen impressed Paul whenever he stepped into it. The dark brown custom cabinets complemented the black and tan granite counters. A six burner stainless steel chef's stove, which Pina, an excellent cook used every day, sat to the right of a large copper sink. To its left blue digital temperature lights glowed above the glass panel on a thirty-five bottle wine cooler.

Paul and Tino sat at the marble-topped table. Pina served two cups of espresso and a plate of biscotti, then left the men alone.

"Ya know," Tino tapped the table, "if my dealership wasn't making so much money, I'd walk away from this shit."

Paul cocked his head and stared at the former Mafia Capo. "What prompted this?"

"Thinking of the old days, and Big Ange."

Please, not him again. "Angelo Ferranti? He died in 2006 ... he was ninety-five."

Tino shrugged. "Yeah, but I dreamed of him last night. He was my goomba ... helped me when I was made and kept me out of trouble. The poor bastard was a good man, but he lost everything."

"So, you owe a dead guy." He set his biscotto on top of the small coffee cup and lifted his hands palms up. "Now you're thinking about leaving?"

"No. Like I said, I'm making too much money. But you know, Ange left this thing you guys created. He walked away, and no one killed him."

Paul smiled. "That's true, but the program has been good to you. Big Ange didn't own a thriving Cadillac dealership. You finished testifying years ago. Your son and his wife run the business, have two good kids, and a big house on the beach. You're straight now. What more do you want?"

"Sometimes it's good to talk of the old days and the guys on my crew. You're the only one I can be honest with."

"Tell me. I go through the same shit every day. You think when people ask me what I do for a living I can tell them?" He picked up the cookie and held it front of him. "Pina makes the best biscotti in the world, but they're not the reason I come here. I visit religiously, every three weeks, so we can talk. There are things we both can't say to anyone else. You're my success story."

Tino nodded. "That's why we get along so well. We're both bullshitting our way through life. It hasn't been easy."

"No, but you did it. You gave up your past. Now you're free."

Tino stared at his cup, then downed his coffee and grinned. "Did I ever tell you the story of the time I pissed on the door handles of an FBI car?"

Paul's eyes widened with his broad smile. "No. Did they deserve it?"

Three hours later, Paul used the code to pass through the gate and enter the Lutz community of Stonebrier, north of Tampa. A year earlier Ammar had collected his reward money from the government and purchased a $450,000 home in the upscale gated neighborhood.

Paul smiled each time he recalled Ammar's exact words when he told him of the purchase. He never forgot that conversation.

Paul, I used my money wisely. I bought a beautiful home in Lutz. It's in Stonebrier ... only thirty minutes from a mosque.

Well congratulations, Ammar. What made you choose that area?

Many people who are close to nature live in nearby communities. The realtor said they are dedicated naturists.

Paul couldn't bring himself tell the devout Muslim that Lutz and Land-O Lakes were loaded with nude and clothing optional communities. There was no reason for him to be the bearer of bad news. Why tell the poor guy that people, in not-too-distant neighborhoods, were cavorting around naked?

Thirty-six-year-old Ammar Bin Rasheed hadn't been the easiest case Paul had undertaken. He was surprised an Italian-American Catholic like himself, got along so well with the former Iranian terrorist.

He pulled into the driveway. By the time he turned off the engine and got out, the garage door opened and Ammar walked to his car.

He bowed and touched his forehead with his right hand. "Salaam. Come, my wife is making coffee."

As always, Paul replied with the Catholic greeting. "Peace be with you." *More coffee, just what I need.* He couldn't refuse, but wasn't looking forward to overly sweet Turkish rocket fuel.

They walked into the minimally furnished, but comfortable, living room and took a seat at a high round table with two wooden stools. A wooden plank coffee table sat in front of a well-used couch and armchair. Against one wall stood an impressive black lacquer cabinet. The double glass panel doors were outlined in mother-of-pearl. Middle Eastern knickknacks, and books titled in Arabic, filled most of the shelves. The top shelf held family photos, taken in Ammar's new American life.

"It has been a long time. Did you get an answer from Mr. Donaldson?" asked Ammar.

Paul nodded. "WITSEC headquarters received a call. He wants to meet with you at CIA Headquarters in Langley, Virginia."

Ammar glanced around the room. "You sure it's about my father?"

"I hope it's an answer to your question about his wellbeing."

"Good. When do I go?"

"Next Wednesday. I'll arrange your flight to Nashville. You and Inspector Hale will fly to Dulles. A few people will meet you there."

A'isha, Ammar's twenty-year-old wife, walked in and set two cups in front of them. Paul had first met her when she was seventeen, a year after she married Ammar. A long black abaya covered her body, a hijab concealed all but her face. Her gaze lowered, she made no eye contact with either man.

Ammar shooed her away with a wave of his hand, and she scurried up a flight of stairs.

Paul took a sip. "Have you heard more from your sister in Greece?"

"Nothing new, but I talk to her once a month."

"Using our system, right?"

"Yes. As I said, she's too frightened to travel to Tehran. I hope they found out our father is well."

"God willing, you will get good news."

After fifteen minutes of small talk about the house and how Ammar was doing, Paul pushed his chair away from the table. "I'll call in the next day or so and tell you when I'll pick you up."

Ammar walked him to his car, and he backed out of the driveway.

###

During the drive back to Tampa, Paul contemplated the two cases. Although he didn't agree with Santino's career choice, he understood the man. La Costa Nostra preyed on people by exploiting their vices. Seldom did their violence fall on the innocent law abiding citizen. Ammar didn't fit into that category. In the past, his ideology didn't distinguish between the innocent and those perceived to be the enemy. *Kill people because of their thoughts and beliefs.*

People don't understand how the government's Witness Security Program could provide assistance to those who had little respect for life. The WITSEC inspectors scattered across the United States had varying degrees of morality, the program itself had none.

CHAPTER V

THE NEW GUY

Forty-nine-year-old Anjoli Landry sat at her desk in WITSEC headquarters. With thirty minutes remaining before she had to leave for a meeting with Social Security officials, she cleared her desk.

Victor Serban stepped into her cubicle. "Hi, Anjoli."

She smiled at him. "Pull up that chair. Are you with us for good now?"

"Yeah. Just finished speaking with John Colombus. He told me you'd fill me in. What's going on in the southeast? How many active cases do we have?"

"I just turned my computer off because I'm going to a meeting. Don't have an exact count, but around eighteen are still getting monthly funding."

"Which offices are busy?"

"Miami, with a big trial, and two more are scheduled in the next month. Atlanta and Tampa are involved with the most active relocated witnesses." She paused. "Did they set up your access to the computers yet?"

"Not until tomorrow."

"This afternoon, when I get back, we'll scan through a few of the cases. I'll point out those that have problems."

Victor stood. "Good." He started to turn and stopped. "Who has single women?"

Anjoli leaned her head to the side and hesitated. *Odd question.* "Two in Atlanta and one in Miami."

"What about the other regions?"

"What they do is none of my business. Why do you ask?"

Victor grinned. "At WITSEC basic training they told us what can happen to a male inspector if he's not careful around a female witness. I don't want any problems in my region. We'll look at the cases later." He walked away.

She bit her lip. *Suddenly the region is the property of the new kid on the block.* She checked to make sure nothing sensitive had been left out, locked the drawers, and picked up her purse.

Anjoli returned at twelve-thirty. During lunch most people went out, eager to relax and get away from work. She turned on her computer and logged in with the new username and password John Colombus had given her. WC-9269, Tatiana Fedorka's confidential file popped onto the screen. After entering the new social security number she made a mental note to send the documentation to Paul. In twenty-four years with WITSEC, she had never been asked to hide a case from the others in the office. She smiled and signed out of Tatiana's file.

Late that afternoon, Victor approached her desk. For the next three hours they discussed each office in the region, and a few cases actively being worked. She did not mention Tatiana Fedorka, formerly Faina Lobanov, and now Tatiana Demko.

It was well past quitting time when she glanced at her watch. "That's it for tonight. I've got a long drive ahead of me, and the traffic shouldn't be bad." She turned off her computer and locked her desk.

Victor stood. "We accomplished quite a bit. Sorry for keeping you late."

While driving home Anjoli kept shaking her head. Victor was going to be a pain in the ass. He had peppered her with detailed and unexpected questions about the witnesses and the inspectors working their cases. Two stuck in her mind. *Why did he keep asking if I showed him all the cases?* She told him she hadn't because they were still waiting on his security clearance upgrade. *Why did he want to know who was the most trusted inspector in the region?* He told her he needed to know who to go to when things turned ugly. *Maybe he's just being thorough.*

CHAPTER VI

THEY KNOW

Victor Serban stood near the bottom of the cascading waterfall in Meridian Hill Park at 16th & W Streets NW in Washington, D.C. At nine-thirty on a Sunday morning the place was nearly empty.

He started up the steps. Three quarters of the way to the top, he stopped, leaned against the short wall to his right, and paused. A man in filthy clothing, and carrying a tattered backpack, limped down the steps. Victor placed his hand over his nose and mouth when he caught the stench of body odor. He waited until the guy had reached the bottom then stuck his hand under the brush overhanging the top of the wall. His muscles stiffened when he didn't make contact with anything. He moved his hand around and sighed with relief when he felt a two inch long plastic tube. He scanned his surroundings, picked it up and shoved it into his pocket.

###

Monday morning, Victor sat at his desk in WITSEC headquarters and took a framed photo of his grandfather from his briefcase. He stared at it and set it on the desk.

From his pocket he removed a small piece of paper and read the words written on it. *She is in Florida.* At that moment his personal cell phone beeped. He retrieved the text.

`I sent you a message.` **He replied.** `I got it yesterday.`

How the hell do they get their information? He taped the note to a blank sheet of paper and fed it into the crosscut shredder next to his desk.

He turned to his computer and used the temporary password Deputy Chief John Colombus had given him to access unclassified cases. He searched the name Anton Novikoff, Tatiana's boyfriend. Anton's witness number, and prisoner number, appeared on the screen. Below it, the Federal Correctional Institution in Sandstone, Minnesota was listed as the place of incarceration. He logged off, pushed away from his desk and relaxed.

Anjoli sat at her desk reading a thick file when Victor approached. "Slide that chair around here and I'll show you one of the big cases we have."

He pushed it beside her and sat. "Who is it?"

"WC-6121. True name, Ammar Mansouri."

He raised his eyebrows. "That's an old number."

"March 2, 2011. A terrorist killed two unarmed US soldiers on a bus in Frankfurt, Germany. He was a member of the terrorist cell in Nuremberg. Mansouri planned the operation. He spilled his guts ... didn't want to face a murder charge in the US."

"What's his relocation area?"

She hesitated. "As soon as your security clearance is upgraded to Top Secret, you'll be able to access the file." She closed the folder.

Victor smiled. "I called this morning. They said it would be done today or tomorrow."

"Good. Once you get it, check with the Deputy Chief to make sure you have access to all the files."

Victor stood. "Do we have any other big cases?"

Anjoli shrugged. "I think of each case as big. People's lives depend on us and the work we do."

"You're right. We'll talk later." He returned the chair to the front of her desk and walked away.

She didn't enjoy keeping secrets from her coworkers, but the Deputy Chief had been adamant about limiting access to Tatiana's file. She dropped the folder into the two-drawer safe, spun the combination dial, and walked to the Deputy Chief's office.

John stood when she came to his door. "Come in, Anjoli. What can I do for you?"

"Victor is settling in and has been asking questions about the relocated witnesses in the southeast. He wanted to know what big cases we have."

"He's itching to get started. His TS will be approved today. After that, the only one you can't mention is Paul's girl in Tampa."

"Everyone in the office can log into the system and still see her file."

John smiled. "True, but not the new one I created. Have you read the old file yet?"

She shook her head. "Not completely."

"I suggest you do. You'll find it comes to a dead end while she was with Mark in Nashville. The last report says she breached her security, was terminated from the Witness Security Program, and her whereabouts are unknown."

Anjoli's eyes widened. "This is serious, isn't it?"

John nodded. "We've never had a witness killed who followed the rules. Do you want the first one to be your case?"

"No, sir."

"You can't even tell people they don't have a need to know. As far as everyone is concerned, she breached her security and is gone. Every entry is to be made in the new secure file. Do what I'm doing. Remember the old Hogan's Heroes TV show?"

She smiled. "Yes."

"Well, use the Sergeant Schultz defense ... I know nothing."

CHAPTER VII

LOVING THE SUNSHINE

Paul checked the time. *Twelve-fifty. Let's see how serious she is.* He knocked on Tatiana's door. After a few seconds he knocked again.

The door swung open, and for a microsecond his eyes widened. Tatiana stood in front of him, soaking wet, with both hands clamped onto a white towel. *Oh shit, it's not long enough!*

"I just got out of the shower ... come in." She turned and scurried toward the bedroom.

With each step, the bottom of the towel bounced against the top half of her pretty ass.

Sure hope that wasn't planned. If it was, I need to get a female inspector in here. Paul made himself comfortable on the couch.

In less than five minutes she walked into the room wearing a sundress and sandals. *Mark was right, she's a man magnet.* Her wet hair was pulled back into a ponytail and tied with a ribbon. She sat in the chair across from him. "Do you always arrive on time?"

"Yes. Are you always late?"

She grinned. "Women are always late ... sometimes on purpose.

Was it?

"What are we going to do today?"

"I made plans that will keep us busy most of the day. The first thing we're doing is going to *Bed Bath and Beyond*."

Tatiana pressed her lips together and scooted to the edge of the chair.

Shit, that didn't sound right. She's trying not to smile.

"Which one first? Shouldn't a bath come before bed? And you must explain what the beyond is."

Paul cleared his throat. His mouth became dry. "It's ... it's a place ... a store—"

She laughed and held up her hand. "I'm only teasing you. Do you need to buy something for your home?"

"No, we're going there for you."

"Me? For what?"

"We're going to buy the longest and widest beach towels we can find."

Tatiana's face turned red. "The white towel?"

He nodded. "Much too short."

She covered her eyes with both hands as she blushed. "Sorry."

He raised his eyebrows. "I didn't mean to embarrass you."

She lowered her hands. "You didn't. I don't want you to think I did it on purpose."

"I don't." He grinned. "If I did, I would have walked out of here."

She sat erect, her gaze darted around the room. "Then what would have happened?"

"I'd arrange for a female inspector to chaperone whenever we meet."

She stared at him and tears filled the corners of her eyes. "Please don't think I'm that type of woman. Both you and Mark have been good to me. I will never hurt you."

"Good. I'll do my best to help you create a new life." He pulled an envelope from his pocket. "You need to sign for your new social security card."

Her eyes brightened. "That means I can open a bank account."

Paul nodded. "After we have something to eat."

###

Paul and Tatiana sat in Cesare's At the Beach, a restaurant not far from where she was staying. They shared a Mozzarella Caprese and drank ice tea.

Paul handed her three brochures of apartment complexes in Clearwater. "Take a look at these. They're in nice areas and have large exercise rooms."

She spent a few minutes thumbing through the pamphlets and slid one in front of him. "This one, the Enclave of Northwood. It is far from the beach?"

"No ... a twenty minute drive. If you like it, we'll see if a one bedroom is available. I also want to take you to look at cars. You can't depend on me to drive you everywhere."

"Can we go see the apartment today?"

Paul nodded. "Sure, later."

"Will you take me to see a Mini? I've always wanted one."

He grinned. "Hopefully we'll be able to find one that's reasonably priced."

Her gaze lingered on him a moment, and she smiled. "I want a new one."

Paul raised his eyebrows. "I don't want to put you into a bad situation. You'll need to pay for it. I can only give you a few thousand for basic transportation." The smile had not left her face.

"I have the money. I sold the Honda I had in Nashville, and I saved a lot over the years."

"You sure?"

"Yes. I want a twin-turbo convertible."

"That may be too expensive and make life more difficult. There are security issues we need to consider." *The price will change her mind.* "Now that you have a social security card in the name Demko, we need to get you a Florida license." He glanced at his watch. "We'll go to the bank first. When we're done, we'll drive to the apartment complex and then discuss the car."

After Paul paid the bill, they walked to his silver Ford Expedition.

Tatiana pointed to the red and white *Boston Strong* tag on the front bumper.

"Why is Boston strong?"

"It's a saying the city adopted after the marathon bombing in 2013."

As he pulled onto Gulfview Boulevard, a black Lincoln Continental, with dark tinted windows, passed in the opposite direction. He glanced at the blue, white, and red license tag in his rearview mirror, but couldn't determine the state.

As they approached the apartment complex, he turned to her. "Your boyfriend ... he's going to be in jail for a few more years."

"Mark told me, but it's not going to last that long."

Paul raised his eyebrows. "Believe me. They won't release him—"

"I'm talking about him and me. Didn't Mark tell you?"

"No. What?"

"I never trusted him. We were apart often when I was dancing and traveling around Europe. When I found out about his life ... where he worked ... who his friends were, everything was a lie. I never loved him. How can you trust someone when they hide their life from you?"

"If you want to end it, have you told him yet?"

"No. I made up my mind just before I moved here."

Paul nodded. When he had scanned her file, he hadn't seen anything about her testifying in any of her boyfriend's cases. Not knowing what was in the U.S. Attorney's files, he wasn't privy to her involvement, or lack of involvement with the Russian mob. *I may have an innocent bystander as my protected witness. Someone who actually knows nothing of her asshole boyfriend's criminal activity.* He recalled only a single case he had where a person who had no knowledge of a crime was placed into the Witness Security Program.

He turned to her and smiled. "We'll discuss Anton another time."

Later that afternoon Paul sat at the desk in his office. He questioned what she had told him. *Is she bullshitting me? Was she a participant in the crimes?* He shook his head. "I don't think so."

He checked the Preliminary Interview and the Memorandum of Understanding. A detailed examination of both documents would lay out the depth of her participation with the Russian mob.

In the Preliminary Interview, he got an answer to the question that had been bouncing around in his head. Tatiana was a non-witness in the Witness Security Program. She was authorized into the program to keep her boyfriend happy. The government needed him to testify against his former associates. Anton was the sole source of information that could put many people away for a long time.

Paul flipped through her file looking for any reports of interviews by the WITSEC psychologists. If she wasn't a witness to a crime, and had no background of criminal activity, she wouldn't fit the profile shared by most protected witnesses.

He scanned through her file a second time and found nothing. He typed a text message to John Colombus.

A minute later his phone beeped, and he looked at the reply. `Yes. Call Fred Gunther. He'll have the report they did on her.`

Paul dialed Fred's number on his secure phone and waited for an answer.

"Gunther."

"Fred, Paul Baldini. Let's go secure."

"Okay."

He listened to the static on the line and its interruption by the 'Line is Secure' announcement.

"Okay on your end, Fred?"

"Yeah. What can I do for you?"

"WC-9269. Did you do a workup on her?

"Hold on a second." After a brief pause Fred continued. "Tatiana Fedorka. Sure did. Since the early eighties we did an assessment on everyone entering the program ... even family members. I have her file in front of me."

"Do you remember her?"

"Definitely made an impression. She's not someone you easily forget. Bright, self-motivated, and extremely pretty. I guess when the FBI dug through the weeds they couldn't come up with something to charge her with. She's a true innocent bystander. Need a copy of the report?"

"No. What was the focus of your assessment?"

"Basically the main question was what she needed to be successful in the program. I addressed the whole individual. Particular services she might need. The best geographical area for relocation. Her wants and desires."

"What did you think of her?"

"Unlike most of our cases where psychopathy is present to some degree, with her there was none. I do recall she was hesitant about entering the program. But I considered her an easy case to work."

"Were there any surprises?"

"Yes. She's well educated and well spoken. I saw no signs of deception, but three things stick in my mind."

"What?"

"If the stone in the ring she was wearing was real, it set her back a wallet full of money. Also I found her to be completely honest and forthcoming. The only negative was that I didn't think she'd last in the program. She's very independent."

"I know."

"Paul, there's one other thing that may become a problem."

"What's that?"

"She was a highly regarded ballerina. She'll never be able to dance again. She'll have to give it up and find something else."

"Maybe she can teach kids."

"I doubt it. It's surprising what a small world professionals live in. We don't know everybody, but everybody knows someone else who might know you."

"You're right."

"Even if she teaches small children, their parents will want to verify the qualifications of the teacher. Do you have her?"

"Yeah, but few people are in the loop, and Colombus wants to keep it that way."

"She should be the easiest case you've ever worked. Is she causing problems?"

"No. Just the opposite. She's the nicest witness I've ever met."

"Good. Anything else I can help you with?"

"No, Fred. Thanks for the info."

"If you're in my area, give me a call. I'll buy you a drink."

"Will do. Take care." He ended the call.

CHAPTER VIII

THE THREAT

Yuri Gorev, the Military Attaché, sat at his solid oak desk in the third floor office at the Washington, D.C., Russian Embassy. Cream-colored walls were accented with a gold crown and chair rail molding. On the wall behind the desk hung a large circular insignia of Russian Special Forces, the Spetsnaz. Crosshairs of a rifle scope were imposed on a blue background outlined in yellow. A black clip-art image of a bat covered the upper part of the crosshairs.

Oleg Vasilev, a GRU agent, sitting in a white antique padded chair in front of the desk, stared at Yuri's impressive uniform. Both men spoke American English without a telltale accent.

Yuri slammed his hand on the desktop. "Anton Novikoff. The bastard stole three million dollars, and he's telling the Americans everything. I wish I had never heard his name. He has no family. The ballerina is our only hope."

Oleg shook his head. "We may not find the money."

"That doesn't bother me, it can be replaced. I hope he loves her enough to quit testifying?"

"And if he doesn't?"

Yuri raised both hands. "Then the situation is hopeless. Let me see the picture."

Oleg slid a photo across the desk.

Yuri lifted it and stared at the picture.

Tatiana, wearing a white sundress, leaned against a palm tree. He glanced back to Oleg. "There are many places with similar trees. How do you know she's in Florida?"

Oleg smiled. "The Sunshine State. Look at the license tag on the car in the background."

"How did you get this picture?"

"Her best friend, a dancer in London, received it a few months ago. Tatiana wanted her to know she was doing well."

Yuri furrowed his brow. "Man or a woman?"

"A Russian ballerina."

"Her name?"

"Inna Ivashin. When Tatiana disappeared, we contacted her. Two of our men explained how important it was for us to find her good friend."

Yuri's expression changed from a frown to a smile. "Did you check the license tag?"

"Yes. The car is owned by a man in Orlando, Harry Wilson."

"So, she's in Orlando?" He handed the picture to Oleg. "Arrange for someone to talk with Harry Wilson. He may know her. After that, contact Victor. Tell him about this ... we need an address. Do you want more men?"

"No, two is enough."

Yuri raised a finger. "Don't bring her here. Don't mention my name and do not harm her. She holds American citizenship, we don't need to create another problem."

Oleg stood. "How much does she know about the organization?"

"Anton always said he told her nothing. Let's hope he wasn't lying. Her name hasn't been on any of the witness lists provided by the Americans. Send a message to our friend."

A week after he began working at WITSEC headquarters, Victor had been cleared for full access to the computer system and files. His personal cell phone vibrated as he walked out of John Colombus' office.

He checked the text message and whispered. "Orlando, get an address." *Where did they get this stuff?*

When he got to his desk, he pulled the computer keyboard in front of him and typed in his user name and password. Once in the system, he entered the name Tatiana Fedorka.

His heart jumped when her file appeared on the screen. It sank when he read the line below her name. "Terminated. Whereabouts unknown." The entry had been made a month ago by Inspector Mark Hale. He brought up the last Field Report Mark had filed and scanned the three short sentences.

Unable to locate WC-9269 since last month when she was presented with the notification that she had been terminated. Her apartment is empty, and phone has been disconnected. It appears she is no longer in the Nashville area.

He examined her file for any new name documentation and discovered she had been provided with a Social Security card in the name Faina Lobanov. He grinned, wrote it on a pad next to his computer, ripped off the page and shoved it into his pocket. It would be an important key to finding her. *Why Orlando when she was in Nashville?* "Where did Faina go?"

Victor stared into space as he tapped the desktop.

When she left Nashville, she may have moved there and contacted someone in Russia. If she needed help, she'd contact the nearest office, or call the eight hundred number. Orlando had been vacant since Inspector Juan Bonilla was promoted and moved to Denver. He reached for the handset of his secure phone.

Paul answered on the fourth ring. "Hello."

"Paulie?" There was a pause.

"Whom are you calling?"

"This is Victor Serban. I'm trying to reach Paul Baldini."

"This is he, Victor. Welcome to the Southeast Region. Don't ever call me Paulie again ... the name is Paul."

"Sorry. I'm getting settled ... wanted to reach out to the guys in the field. You can call me if there's a problem. Let's go secure."

Paul pressed the button on the phone and waited for the computerized voice to announce the line was secure.

"You there?" Paul asked.

"Yes."

"You'll hear from Bob before you and I speak. I call him when things turn to shit."

"Bob?"

"My boss. Chief Inspector Bob Plummer, in Miami."

"Good, but please remember I'm available. What do you think is the most difficult part of your job?"

Jesus, this guy is green. "Lying and becoming a better con man than the cons."

"What do you mean?"

"You can't tell anyone what you do for a living. You make up shit. That's not conducive to making friends. Then there's the ability to recognize when your witness is playing games."

"Playing games?"

I can tell he hasn't spent much time with relocated witnesses. "People that come into the program are looking to gain an advantage. Inspectors are good targets. Witnesses will do anything to set them up ... get the inspector in a compromising situation. Once a thumb is on him, they get what they want."

"I see what you mean. Do you have any single female cases, or any that are a problem?"

Paul furrowed his brow. *By now he should have figured out which cases are his responsibility.* "No. My newest guy arrived last month ... a long time drug dealer out of Baltimore. He's a pain in the ass, but I've got a handle on it."

"How's he doing?"

"Not well. Most of his life was spent on the streets selling drugs for a trafficker. I asked him if he had any job skills. He said he didn't, but told me he was a magician."

"What are you doing with him?"

Paul took a deep breath. "Not much work performing magic around here unless you're extremely good at it. After I found out he couldn't make himself disappear, I put him in a training program for auto mechanics."

"Smart move."

That went right over his head.

"Ever had any single female cases?"

"One, a few years back. She testified against her ex-husband. She's a real estate agent in Tampa and doing well."

"I feel sorry for the guys that work those cases."

"Don't. Proficiency comes before sympathy in the dictionary. If people can't handle the job, they need to find one in the Marshals Service that's less stressful."

"You're right. If I can help you, call me. We'll talk again later. Stay safe."

The line went dead.

Paul shook his head. "It'll take time for him to figure out what a Case Manager does for a living." *Guess I better go easy on him.*

He dialed the Miami Metro number and Maria answered.

"Hi Maria, Bob there?"

"Yes, hold on."

Paul opened a note pad and scanned the page.

Bob was breathing heavy when he spoke. "What's going on?"

"You okay? Been working out?"

"Yeah, weights."

"I just got off the phone with the new Case Manager."

"You didn't screw with him did you?"

"No, why?"

Bob lowered his voice. "I want to be the first one to drive him bat-shit for a day."

Paul laughed. "By my guest. It won't be difficult. I've got a couple of questions ... you have time."

"Sure."

Their conversation continued after the secure line announcement.

"Is everything okay," Bob asked.

"Yes. You talk to Colombus about my ballerina?"

"Yeah, why?"

"Nothing in her file indicates she has money, but she does."

"So? She could have saved while she was dancing."

"Could be, but I doubt it."

"Why is that?"

Paul glanced at his notes. "Last week she picked an apartment, and we put down a deposit. The same day I provided her a social security card, she opened a bank account. She then told me she wanted to buy a new Mini convertible ... a twin turbo."

Bob laughed. "She's nuts. We don't buy new cars."

"No, but she can ... said she has the money."

"You're talking about a car that cost at least thirty-five thousand dollars. She'll never get qualified for a loan. If they check her background, it will come up empty. That's when they'll start asking questions."

"I explained that to her. She told me everything would be fine ... she's paying cash."

"Right! I collect a few bucks each month, and I don't pay cash for new cars. How much money does a ballerina make?"

"That's the reason I called. Thought you might have that information."

"Me? Christ! I don't own a fucking tutu. Talk with her and call me. Keep it quiet. We're not going to speculate and put it in writing yet. Is that it?"

"No. The HK MP7 you gave me to test fire. Can I hold on to it for a while?"

"Sure. How many forty round mags did I give you?"

"Five."

"Need more?"

"If that's not enough, I'm in deep shit."

CHAPTER IX

SECURITY BREACH

Victor remained in his office well past quitting time. He glanced at his watch. "Damn, nine-forty-five."

On his way out of the office he stopped at Anjoli's desk. He pulled on the drawers and turned to pull open the two drawer safe. She had locked everything. As he started to leave his eyes stopped on a legal pad on the side of the desk. The paper was scored with an indentation where something had been written on a page that had been torn from the pad. He picked it up, looked at it from different angles, and ripped off the sheet.

Victor hurried back to his office, sharpened a pencil, and with the side of the lead began to rub it back and forth over the impressions. He read the words outlined on the paper. "Call Paul about her documentation."

Victor stared at the words. *One inspector in the region is named Paul ... claims he has no female cases.* He turned on his computer and looked at the list of active cases in Tampa.

He mumbled. "No women. Might be documentation for a wife, or an old case."

He sat back. *Maybe not.*

Oleg shook his head as he walked into Yuri's office and stopped in front of the large executive desk.

"You're back from Orlando?" Yuri asked.

"Yes. I talked to the man who owns the car. He doesn't know her. He recalls taking his grandchildren to lunch at a restaurant near where the photo was taken."

"Did you speak with anyone in the restaurant?"

"Yes. The manager. He showed her picture to the waitresses. No one recognized her."

Yuri nodded. "You said Victor gave you her new name?

"Yes. Faina Lobanov. He said she was in Nashville, but has disappeared."

"Anything else?"

Oleg grinned. "Yes, he said she might be in Tampa."

"Who is the witness security agent there?"

"A guy named Paul Baldini."

"I'll have our people downstairs look into his background. We'll see what they find out. Once they're finished, plan another trip to Florida."

71

"Yes, sir." He spun around and headed to the door.

"One more thing, Oleg. Don't harm anyone unless it is necessary. A dead girl is worthless, and if you injure the agent, every cop in America will be looking for you."

Oleg nodded and left the room.

Tatiana sank into the new leather couch. From the white marble coffee table, she picked up a felt *Crown Royal* bag. She loosened the gold tasseled drawstring, poured four diamonds into her hand, and placed it on the table. With her pinky, she rolled the stones around her palm, chose two, and returned the other two to the bag. She held them up and smiled at the light reflecting off their perfect facets. *Flawless and over two carats each. Possibly sixty thousand dollars.*

Tatiana placed the diamonds in a tiny satin jewelry pouch and put it in her pocket. She picked up the *Crown Royal* bag and walked to her bedroom. As she put it into her dresser drawer, the doorbell rang.

Paul hadn't seen Tatiana since the day she negotiated a good price for the new Mini convertible. Once she made up her mind, she had given the salesman two thousand dollars he had provided her. Somehow she arranged to pick up the car the following afternoon. *How did that happen?*

He saw it for the first time when he pulled into the parking lot outside her apartment. The Mini was loaded with every option offered. *She couldn't have paid cash.* He rang the bell.

When Tatiana opened the door, she had on a pair of red shorts and a long sleeved man's shirt.

He grinned. "Hi. You look nice."

"Thank you." She turned in a circle. "See, I'm ready. Come in."

As he entered the living room, his eyes widened. The place looked as if it had been furnished by a professional designer. The tan leather couch and oversized chair were arranged in front of a square coffee table that appeared to be a single solid stone. The table sat on a black rug outlined with large Greek Key symbols. Two matching marble end tables, with cut glass lamps, book-ended the couch.

He looked at the kitchen and a glass table with four white leather chairs. "This isn't the furniture that was in here when you rented the apartment."

She shrugged. "I told them to take everything out and bought my own. Come and look at the bedroom."

He followed her and stopped in the doorway.

"How do you like it? It's the new smart bed. It automatically adjusts to my body."

Paul smiled. *More white!* He pointed to the dresser, end tables, and the black comforter on the queen sized bed. "I guess black and white are your favorite colors."

"They are. Let's go to the living room."

Once they were seated, she wasted no time getting to the point. "You look concerned. Is there a problem with what I bought? What you give me for rent, food, and the things I want is nothing. I have my own money."

He raised his hand. "Don't be angry. No one told me that when you came into the program you were financially sound. Your wellbeing is my responsibility. Financial background checks can cause problems. I don't want anything to happen to you."

Tatiana nodded and leaned back. "Sorry. I thought you knew."

"What?"

"I had over eighty thousand dollars in the bank in Nashville. I closed the account and gave Mark a check for seventy two thousand. The rest I took in cash. He said he'd have the check transferred to my new name. I guess that hasn't been done yet."

Paul stared at her and raised his eyebrows. "I'm sorry. No one told me. I should have been notified."

"An innocent mistake. I don't need the money today. Good ballerinas are paid well. For many years I lived the life of a nun ... saved as much as I could. Those days have ended." She grinned. "Have you ever been to Amsterdam?"

"Yes, a couple of times."

"Did you visit any of the diamond factories?"

"Sure did. Right after a tour of the Heineken Beer Museum ... the Royal Asscher Diamond Company. It's not far from the museum."

She took the satin pouch from her pocket, opened it, and held up a diamond. "That's where Anton bought this for me." She dropped the stone into his palm.

Paul moved the diamond across his hand. "This is over a carat."

"It's a little over two."

"I bought two half carat stones from Royal Asscher." He handed it back to her. "What they sell is high quality, and not cheap. I still have those two stones."

She pointed at his hand. "They're not in a ring?"

"No. Earrings for my wife."

Tatiana stared at him for a full five seconds before she spoke. "What happened to her?"

He took a deep breath. "She died in a plane crash five years ago."

Her eyes widened. She put her hand over her mouth and didn't say a word for a moment. When she lowered it, she said, "I'm truly sorry."

"Thank you. I try to not think about it." He pointed at the diamond. "Why are you carrying it around in your pocket?"

"I got a safe deposit box at the bank. I want to put it there."

"Good idea. I came today to ask if you've thought about finding a job."

"I don't think I'll ever be able to dance professionally again, but I'd like to teach ballet."

Paul nodded. "I want to be honest with you. Dancing is out of the question, and teaching ballet may pose a problem."

"Why?"

"There are ways to create a background, but it could never relate back to anything you've done. A qualified teacher must promote what she did ... where she performed. You'll never be able to speak of your past."

"It's been my whole life. Not being able to dance will hurt, but thankfully I've saved as much money as I could."

"I'll call Mark about the check. WITSEC headquarters should have finished getting the funds transferred to your new name." He stood. "I better be going."

She led him to the door, turned before she opened it, and took his hand. "Thank you for everything."

He pulled his hand from hers and placed it on her shoulder. "You're welcome. Now go to the bank and drop that diamond in the box."

After Paul left her apartment, Tatiana went to the bank. She stood in the safe deposit vault.

A clerk set the box on a table in front of her. "Call me when you're finished."

She waited until he had left the vault and took the *Crown Royal* bag from her purse. She placed the bag in the center of her hand. The weight brought a smile to her face. "Converting the cash to diamonds was smart, Anton. Giving them to me was a mistake. You should have buried them." She dropped the bag into the box, picked it up, and called the clerk.

After he had left Tatiana, Paul walked into his office and called Mark. They waited for a secure connection.

"Why didn't you tell me WC-9269 had money? She said she's waiting for a check to be cleared by headquarters."

"Damn, Paul. I'm sorry. Colombus had me delete quite a few reports from her file before I sent it to you. I meant to tell you, but it slipped my mind."

"Okay, no sweat. Who is working on the check?"

"Anjoli. It should be done by now. Want me to call her?"

"No. I will. I spent an hour with Tatiana this morning. She purchased a new Mini convertible and an apartment full of expensive furniture. She paid cash for the car and I'll bet did the same to furnish her place."

Mark didn't reply.

"You still with me, Mark?"

"Yeah. She left here with over nine thousand in her purse."

"That doesn't come close to covering the furniture, much less the car. Did she go through TSA Security?"

"Yes. A cop and I watched her. If anyone saw a pile of money, they didn't question it."

"It doesn't add up. Nine grand is forty-one thousand short. We're talking about a new car, and a one bedroom apartment full of top-of-the-line furniture."

"She couldn't have financed any of it."

Paul shook his head. "No. Financially, she's a ghost. No one is going to approve a loan for her."

"Did she explain how she did it?"

"No. She said she has her own money, and I believe she may have access to it."

"Come on, Paul. You don't just walk around with over fifty thousand in cash in your purse. That's five hundred C-Notes."

"Shit. I don't want to get headquarters involved yet, but I should call Miami and bring the boss up to date."

After the call, Paul drove home, dropped off his government car and left in his Cadillac CTS. He went to Jimmy's Crows Nest on the tenth floor of the Pierhouse 60 Hotel at Clearwater Beach.

A few tourists sat at tables admiring the view, but there was no crowd at this early hour. Paul took an empty stool at the end of the bar.

The bartender stepped in front of him. "Hi, Paul. Which usual do you want?"

"You staying out of trouble, Diego?"

"As best I can."

"Good. Give me the 'driving my Cadillac' special."

Diego pulled a bottle of Skyy vodka from the shelf and poured two shots into a tall glass of ice. He added tonic water and placed the drink in front of Paul. "Skyy, tonic water not soda, and no fruit."

"That's it." He smiled and set twelve dollars on the bar.

Diego looked at a man leaning against the bar. "Be back in a second."

When Diego walked away, he stared at his drink for a good fifteen seconds. He shook his head. *Drinking alone again. This sucks.*

Diego returned and lowered his voice. "How's business at the Marshals Office?"

"Great. I'm keeping a low profile and chasing bad guys. School going okay?"

Diego smiled. "My last year. A masters in Police Administration should make life easier."

"Call me when you start handing out your resume. I'll put in a good word for you."

The young bartender leaned toward him. "I'm going to try to stick to a uniformed service. I can't see how you guys work undercover, keep your job chasing fugitives' secret, and live a normal life."

He shook his head. "If you only knew. It's not easy keeping things quiet, and on top of that worrying about a dirtbag you arrested going after your family. Stick to administration and work your way to the top. You'll be much happier."

Diego glanced as a couple took seats at the bar. "You going to have a second one?" he asked Paul.

"No. One's enough." He slid the money to Diego. "Thanks."

"Anytime."

Paul watched him walk to the other end of the bar. *Smart kid. Stay away from the jobs where ninety percent of the time you need to lie about what you do for a living.*

When he saw Tatiana walking toward him, his heart jumped.

Her wide leg black pants flowed with the breeze off the Gulf. The teal top exposed a few inches of her taut midriff. Her hair, falling over her left shoulder, was tied with a teal ribbon.

He looked at Diego. The young man's eyes were wide, mouth half open, and head bobbed with each click of her heels on the tile floor. The guy sitting on the barstool in front of him was so intent on watching her, he almost knocked over his drink.

She placed her hand on the stool next to him. "This is a pleasant surprise. May I join you, Paul?"

I don't want to be a jerk and leave. I'll ride it out and write a report. "Please do."

After she sat, he leaned to her. "How did you know about this place?"

"When I was staying at the resort, I met a girl at the pool and she brought me here for lunch. I love the view."

"Did you drive?"

"No. I'll be drinking so I took a cab. I remember you telling me the police are always looking for people who drink and drive."

Diego hurried over to them. "Who's your friend, Paul?"

"Tatiana." He glanced at her and motioned the bartender. "This is, Diego. The best bartender on the beach."

She smiled. "Nice to meet you. May I have a vodka tonic with one olive?"

Diego looked at Paul and then back at Tatiana. "Skyy?"

"No. Stolichnaya."

"Wow. A lot of people drink it, but few pronounce it correctly." He removed a quart bottle from a shelf and mixed her drink.

"Run me a tab," Paul said.

Diego nodded. "You two are friends?"

"Yeah. Tatiana and I met at an animal shelter fundraiser. We both love dogs."

"What's your favorite breed?" he asked her.

"The Papillon."

"Nice choice. Enjoy your drink." He walked away to take care of other customers.

Paul turned to her and kept his voice low. "You know this could cause problems."

"What?"

"Us. In a bar having a drink together."

"Who's going to find out?"

"The Marshals Service."

She looked at him with a lost child's expression on her face. "You think I will tell them?"

"Actually, no I don't."

She grinned. "Good. Then let's enjoy ourselves and not talk about your job."

I stepped in it. I may as well jump in with both feet. "Good. Tell me how life was as a prima ballerina."

She laughed. "I get to teach you something. Many years ago the highest ranked ballerina was a Prima Ballerina Assoluta. In most companies today the highest rank is Principal Dancer. Below that is First Soloist, then Demi-Soloist, and last Corps de Ballet."

"And of course you were a Principal Dancer."

"Yes. A year before I left dancing, I reached that level."

"Do you regret leaving and being dragged into the situation you're now in?"

"Yes and no. I love ballet, but it's a hard life filled with physical injuries. It would be difficult to return to the pain and stress a performing ballerina must face."

"Then what do you want in life?"

"A family, and one day to teach ballet. Tell me about your wife."

"Her name was Celeste."

"From the Latin word *caelestis* meaning heavenly, or a god-like person."

"Yes, and she was."

"Where was she born?"

"In Boston. We met when she was a freshman and I was a senior at Boston College. Do you also speak Latin?"

"No, but words in many languages derive from Latin."

'You said you speak six languages. How do you stay proficient in them?"

She laughed. "You're going to think I'm crazy."

"No I won't."

"When I ask myself a question, or just think about something, I do it in different languages. Now you know my secret, I talk to myself in Ukrainian, and answer in French or Italian."

He smiled and nodded. "I don't think that's crazy. It's a good system. Sometimes I think in Italian."

"You do?"

"Whenever someone does something stupid, an Italian cussword comes to mind."

They talked for the next hour and then left the bar.

He pulled into a parking place near her apartment. "Did you enjoy yourself?"

"Yes. Will you walk me to the door?"

He hesitated.

She smiled. "Don't worry. I won't ask you in."

He winked at her and got out of the car.

Tatiana unlocked the door. "Thank you for not treating me like a client or your patient. You're a gracious gentleman."

He nodded. "I'll call you in the morning."

CHAPTER X

SOMEONE IS WATCHING

Paul pressed the garage door remote as he pulled in front of his two-story condo. He had purchased the two-bedroom unit at The Village on Harbor Island a year after his wife died. Remaining in the home they had lived in together was out of the question. It was too big and brought back too many memories. Good times ended when the plane crashed.

The move from a large single family house, to the seventeen-hundred square foot condo, hadn't been easy. Since garage sales weren't his thing, The Salvation Army had made out like bandits. Renovations to the kitchen, installing hardwood floors, and redoing both of the bathrooms had taken four months. Paul didn't consider himself a perfectionist, but when the contractor finished, he half-jokingly told him to never call again.

He parked the government SUV beside his Cadillac and closed the garage door.

Once inside, he walked to his upstairs bedroom and stepped to the dresser. He stared at the photo of Celeste. "It's been over five years, darling. I miss your voice, your smile, and your warm body next to mine." He wiped his eyes and placed his fingers on his wife's image. "I want a normal life again ... someone I can talk to when the stress and loneliness of this job raises its ugly head. Please understand when I say I need to move forward. I need to live again."

The doorbell rang. He walked down the steps, opened the door and smiled at his seventy-five-year-old next door neighbor. "Hi Harold." He moved out of the doorway. "Come in. Want a drink?"

"No. Harrietta and I are on our way to see a movie. She's dragging me to see the one named after that asshole Johnson's wife. It's some kind of going age female feature."

Paul bit the side of his cheek to keep from laughing. "*Lady Bird*. It's a coming-of-age chick flick. It's actually not about the president's wife."

"Good, he was a jerk. I wanted to let you know someone was knocking on your door today. He was driving a big Chevrolet SUV. Stood in front of your door for so long I came out and told him you were at work."

"You get his name?"

"No, but he had an odd accent."

"Probably trying to sell something."

"I did get the tag number when he drove away." He pulled a small piece of paper from his pocket and handed it to Paul.

He looked at it. "You sure it was Fulton County?"

Harold smiled. "Couldn't miss it. Harrietta and I lived outside Atlanta for ten years."

"Thanks, Harold. Good investigative work."

Harold nodded. "I called the U.S. Marshals office. They said you didn't work there."

Damn, here we go again. He smiled. "I guess I never explained. I'm not associated with the local Marshals office. I work for Marshals Service Headquarters ... organized crime cases."

Harold frowned. "They gave me an 800 number to call, but the guy who answered wasn't Mr. Friendly. He started asking personal questions. Wanted to know what my WC number was. What the hell was he talking about?"

"I have no idea."

"All he did was question me. I got angry and asked him if he was trying to become a beneficiary on my life insurance policy. Didn't wait for his reply, I hung up."

"I'm sorry, Harold. I'll give you my cell number. Did the guy who came to the door ask about me?"

"No. Didn't even say goodbye, he just left. I'll bet he was related to the jerk that answered the 800 number. Wish the association would keep solicitors out of the neighborhood."

"When I retire I'll put in for the job of community enforcer."

Harold grinned. "I'll nominate you and Harrietta will second the motion."

They talked for a few minutes, then Paul walked him to the door. "Don't let it bother you. Everyone wants to stick their nose in other people's business."

After he closed the door, he walked to the liquor cabinet and poured himself a Scotch. *More lies to hide what I do for a living. And they wonder why we can't keep friends.* He headed upstairs to the extra bedroom. It not only served as his home office, but a place to relax in front of a sixty-inch television. A large bookcase, and a shelf along a wall held trophies he won in state and national shooting competitions.

He dropped the paper Harold had given him on his desk, punched a number into his cell phone and tapped the speaker icon.

"Pinellas County Sheriff's Office."

"This is U.S. Marshal Paul Baldini. I need to run a tag."

"Hold on, please."

After a few seconds a woman answered. "Please verify your InterCity call sign, Inspector Baldini."

"Metro 703."

"And your Marshals Service badge number?"

"One-two-one-one."

After a short pause the woman asked, "What is the tag number?"

"Georgia, Bravo Zulu Zulu 0892. It's Atlanta ... Fulton County."

"Standby."

He slid the notepad in front of him and picked up the pen.

"Sir?"

"Yes."

"A 2015 black Chevy Tahoe. It's registered to Atlanta South Security Services. You need the address?"

"Yes, please."

"4275 Jonesboro Road, Union City, Georgia 30291."

"Thank you."

"Anytime." The line went dead.

He ripped the page from the pad, folded it and slid it into his wallet.

###

At his office the next morning, Paul called Bob Plummer and established a secure line.

"What's up?" Bob asked.

"Odd things are happening."

"Like what?"

"A week or so ago I spotted a blacked-out Lincoln Continental near where Tatiana was staying. Out-of-state tag … might have been DC."

"So?"

"Yesterday my neighbor said a guy was knocking on my door so he walked over to talk to him. Said he had an accent, and wasn't friendly, so he got his tag number."

"You're not giving me much to go on. You want to write it up and send it to me?"

"No. I ran the tag. Need you to look into the company listed on the registration. Ask Colombus to use his connections to check on them. It a 2015 Tahoe registered to Atlanta South Security Services, 4275 Jonesboro Road, Union City, Georgia, 30291."

"Got it. Ever seen it in your neighborhood before?"

"No. Let's see what John can find out."

"Okay, give me twenty-four hours. Is that it?"

"No. I don't want to put this in writing yet. I think my ballerina has a stash of money, and it's quite large."

He told his boss about the new car, new furniture, and the diamond she had shown him.

"Damn," Bob said. "That's a problem. If she's getting money from someone, it's a security breach."

"True, but I'm good a reading people. I think she brought the money with her."

"How much are we talking about?"

Paul chuckled. "Beats the shit out of me. If I had to guess, I'd say well into six figures."

"With airport security the way it is today, people don't fly with that much cash stashed in their luggage."

"That's what bothers me. How the hell did she do it? Then again, it won't matter if her spending stops. I'll do the Italian thing ... forget-about-it."

"You want to confront her?"

Paul hesitated. "I will, but let's see if she keeps buying things like a drunk sailor. If she does, we may need to move her to Miami."

"Okay, keep me informed. As soon as you talk to her, call me."

"I'll visit her in the morning, but I don't think she'll admit to having that much cash."

"If she's smart, she won't." Bob hesitated. "On another subject. What are you doing today?"

"Going to the range."

"If I was there, I'd go with you. Don't shoot yourself in the foot. Anything else you need to tell me?"

"Yeah. I'm sending you a report about an after-hour meeting with her."

"What happened?"

"I was having a drink in a bar at the beach and she walked in the place."

"And you walked out, right?"

"No. We talked for an hour."

"Jesus. You should have paid the bill and left."

"By-the-book, right? This job is difficult enough without putting more strain on my attempts to help people assimilate into a new life. Why do we need to be assholes and run away from a chance encounter with one of our witnesses?"

"Personal relationships are a path to accusations."

"Who said it was personal? We talked about the years she spent dancing, and what she might want to do in the future. It's what I do for a living ... establish professional relationships."

"What if she says you got drunk?"

"What if Chicken Little's sky falls? I know my witness, and I cover my ass. If management doesn't trust my instincts why are they sending me high profile cases?"

"You have a point there."

"I don't intentionally break the rules, but I'm not going to treat any of my cases like they're walking around with a severe form of leprosy. A certain amount of trust is needed to turn a relocated witness into an upstanding member of society."

"People in headquarters sometimes don't understand."

"That's an understatement. I can think of one or two who need to get their asses out in the field and work a relocation case."

"You're right. We'll log it as work time spent assessing the needs of the witness."

"Thanks, Bob. You understand how difficult this job can be, and I appreciate it."

"I do. Any other surprises?"

"Not today, and hopefully not anytime soon."

"Good. Keep me up-to-date."

"I will." He ended the call.

CHAPTER XI

DIAMONDS

Paul left his condo at ten the next morning. As he turned onto Windward Way, he noticed the black Tahoe parked in front of the local marina.

Think you can tail me? I'm not going anywhere until I ditch your ass. He drove the short distance to Clearwater Memorial Causeway and turned left. Once he crossed the bridge, he came to South Ft. Harrison Avenue in downtown Clearwater. He took another left. *Scientology has the best video surveillance in Florida, and these assholes must know it.*

Just south of the Ft Harrison Hotel he turned into a parking lot, took the first vacant space and got out of his Ford Expedition. Under the watchful eyes of church cameras, he saw the Tahoe drive past the front entrance of the hotel.

Within seconds of entering the hotel a young woman in black slacks and a white shirt stepped in front of him, blocking any further movement.

"May I help you, sir?"

"Possibly."

She hesitated and frowned. "Who are you with?"

He looked around, motioned behind him, and smiled. "As you can see, I'm alone. I drove over from Miami today." He glanced across the ornate lobby. "I think I may be in the wrong place."

"Sir, this is the Church of Scientology. We can help you travel to higher states of spiritual awareness. Our auditors are experts at helping people locate areas of spiritual distress in their lives."

He smiled. "Well, the only distress I'm experiencing is having relied on memory, and not turning on the lady in the box."

With a stern look on her face, she cocked her head to the side. "You have a lady in a box?"

"Yeah, the GPS in my car. The little spirit has a lovely voice. Sorry to bother you. Have a good day." He turned and walked out of the hotel.

On his way to his car, he glanced in both directions. The Tahoe was gone.

While driving to Tatiana's apartment he stayed off the main roads. A single vehicle trying to follow him would be easy to spot on small residential streets.

###

Paul pulled into a parking space fifty feet from Tatiana's apartment. While walking to her door he scanned the area.

After what had happened during past visits, he was apprehensive. He pressed the doorbell. *Please be dressed.* He took a deep breath.

The door swung open. *Jeans and a T-shirt ... thank you, God.*

"Come in." She headed to the living room, sat at one end of the couch, and tapped the cushion beside her. "Sit with me."

He sat against the armrest at the opposite end.

She tucked her legs under her. "What do you want to talk to me about?"

"Your money situation. You paid cash for the car. How did you pay for the furniture?"

"Cash."

"Tatiana, we need to be honest with each other. I can't keep you safe and help you assimilate into your new life if you're hiding something."

"What do you think I'm hiding from you?"

The last time they spoke, she had changed the subject from her expensive purchases to the diamond her boyfriend had bought. He would not let it happen again.

"Mark said you came here with under ten thousand dollars. You haven't received the money from the check you gave him. How did you pay for the car," he waved his hand across the room, "and this new furniture?"

She smiled. "I thought I explained ... Anton bought me diamonds when we were in Amsterdam."

He furrowed his brow and paused. "You showed me one two carat stone. That doesn't explain where you got the money to pay for everything."

Tatiana scooted closer to him and shrugged. "I guess I should have made it clearer. He didn't buy one diamond, he bought me six. I sold three of them to a jeweler here in Clearwater." She got off the couch, "Wait. I'll get the receipt." She marched to her bedroom.

When she returned, she handed Paul a folded paper and sat on the center cushion.

He scanned the page and recognized the name of the store. His eyes locked on the dollar figure at the bottom. "They paid you ninety-one thousand dollars for three stones?"

"Yes. They are IF, D clarity, and over two carats."

"Don't take this the wrong way. How did the jeweler verify they weren't stolen?"

She leaned to him and placed her hand on his thigh. "I don't. You've been good to me." She removed her hand. "You don't know much about diamonds, do you?"

He shook his head "No, I don't. Enlighten me."

Tatiana grinned. "You'll be my student, and again I'll be your teacher. The stones you bought in Amsterdam, were they generic or Royal Asscher Cut?"

He shook his head and furrowed his brow. "I can tell you they were expensive."

"The ones I have are their best. Every Royal Asscher Cut diamond has two laser inscriptions on it. The first is the unique serial number, which is stored in their database, and the second is the Royal Asscher logo. The jeweler called them and they verified the purchase."

"In whose name were they bought?"

"Anton Novikoff's."

"Okay. How did they know you didn't take them from Anton?"

"The jeweler made a video call. I was with Anton when he bought them. The salesman recognized me."

Paul's muscles tightened, and he sat up. "Do you know what you just did?"

She shook her head. "Am I in trouble?"

"I don't know yet. You may have breached your security." He took a moment to pull his thoughts together. "Were Anton's friends told he bought the diamonds?"

"No. He didn't want anyone to find out how much money he had saved. Anton even gave the salesman a fake address in Belarus and told him to never discuss what he bought with anyone except us. The man at Asscher wasn't going to verify anything with the jeweler until I spoke to him and said it was okay."

"For now we won't worry about it. Don't ever do that again without discussing it with-me first."

She gave him a quick hug and leaned back. "Thank you."

"Do you have any idea what one of those stones sells for in a jewelry store?"

She nodded and raised her eyebrows. "About $60,000.00. I hated to sell them so cheap."

###

Three hours later Paul sat at his desk. He avoided going to the office as much as possible, but he needed a secure phone. Bob had told him to call after speaking to Tatiana. The one thing that worried him was that her picture had been sent halfway across the world. Anton couldn't receive, or make international phone calls from the jail. Paul doubted the people at Royal Asscher Diamonds would release information on their customers.

He got Bob on the phone.

"I talked to her this morning. I don't think there's anything we need to worry about."

"You sure, Paul? Where the hell did she get the money?"

"Remember the diamond I told you she showed me?"

"Yeah."

"Well, there's more than one. Her boyfriend bought her six large stones. She sold three of them."

"Without any questions being asked?"

Paul had anticipated the question. "If you owned a jewelry store, and a recently divorced woman came in to sell her diamonds at a good price, would you question her?" He waited for a response.

"No. I'd buy them."

"Me too." Paul had to change the subject and quit talking about diamonds. "Did you tell John why you wanted to check out the company in Atlanta?"

"No."

"Good. Did he get back to you yet?"

"No. I'll call and light a fire under his ass. If it's necessary, move her to a hotel. Give me a buzz if you need funds, I'll get the approval."

Paul hesitated. "If things continue to happen, I'm sure that's what I'll do. You'll be the first one to hear about it."

"Okay. Keep me informed."

"I will. Talk to you later." He ended the call, locked his desk and headed out of the office.

CHAPTER XII

QUESTIONS

Angoli saw the note on her desk and walked to Victor's office. "You wanted to see me?"

"Yeah. I talked to Paul Baldini the other day. I called him Paulie."

Anjoli's mouth dropped open and her eyes widened. "Tell me you didn't."

"I guess that was a mistake."

"I should have warned you. There are people who call Bob Plummer, Bobbie. A few call Mark Hale, Markie. No one calls Paul, Paulie."

"What's the big deal?"

"Only his wife called him that."

"Called? Past tense?"

Anjoli nodded. "Yes. She was one of twelve people killed in a plane crash in August 2011. It was in Canada."

"Jesus, that's too bad. I'll call and apologize."

She held up her hand. "Don't. Let it go. He doesn't need to be reminded of what happened. You want to stay on his good side. He's the best asset you have in the region. If you want something done right ... call Paul."

"How well do you know him?"

"Quite well. His wife and I both attended Boston College."

"Were you friends?"

"Although we didn't go there at the same time, we became friends."

"Someone told me Mark Hale and Paul are competitive shooters. Are they friends?"

She furrowed her brow. *Jesus. This guy bounces from subject to subject.* "Yes. Do you shoot competitively?"

"No, but one day I'd enjoy watching them."

John Colombus sat at his desk. He answered his phone on the second ring.

"Colombus."

"John, Ed Franklin. Got some information on the company you asked me to check out."

"I can always rely on the FBI. What did you find?"

"Atlanta South Security Services ... a big company. It's owned by Sean O'Brien, an Irishman with connections in New York."

"What connections?"

"The mob. Specifically the Russian mob. Many of his employees' names end in p-o-v, or n-o-v. We're keeping an eye on the contracts they're trying to secure. Is there something we can do for you?"

"No. It's nothing. Our guys in Atlanta saw one of their cars parked near the federal courthouse. An employee could have gotten himself in a jam. Thanks for the help."

"No problem. Let me know if the FBI can help."

"I will. Take care." He stared across the office wondering why Bob wanted information on an Atlanta security company. *He may have found out they are working a job in Miami?* After the call, he made a note to contact Bob in the morning.

Anjoli knocked on his doorframe. "You busy, Chief?"

"No, have a seat."

She sat on the couch across from his desk and frowned. "Something is bothering me."

"What?"

"I've been with WITSEC a long time ... twenty-four years. I remember many of the old guys who worked witnesses before the 1984 Crime Control Act was passed. Today the government would put them in jail for things they did."

"That's bothering you?"

"No. It's Victor. He's been asking odd questions. Earlier today he asked about Mark Hale and Paul."

"What did he want?"

"Nothing really. Made a comment about them both being competitive shooters. The one thing that was odd is he wanted to know about single female witnesses."

John hesitated and rubbed his chin. "That's innocent enough. I wouldn't worry."

"You're right, Chief. He's new and inquisitive." She stood. "Thanks for listening."

After she left his office, John hit the speaker button on his phone, dialed, and waited for an answer.

"Information Technology, Les."

"Lester, John Colombus. I need you to do something for me for the next two weeks."

"Sure, what is it?"

"Can you track what a person is looking at on the WITSEC computers?"

"If I have their user name and password."

"Can you put it in the form of a written report?"

"Yes, but you'll need to give me access to your system."

"No problem. When's a good time for you to come up to my office?"

"I'll come up now?"

"Great. I'll be waiting. One more thing. Don't tell anyone in WITSEC, or in your shop, about this."

"I won't."

CHAPTER XIII

TACTICS

Oleg sat at a table in his room at the Hilton Clearwater Beach Resort. With him were Dmitry and Pavel. Both men had worked at Atlanta South Security Services for two years.

Oleg hadn't had much luck following Paul around Clearwater. He stared across the room and turned back to the two men. "This cop knows we're watching him."

"He's protected witnesses for many years. I don't think he is stupid," Dmitry said.

Pavel raised his hand. "That may be so, but he doesn't know who we are. Who told you this girl is living in Tampa?"

Oleg clamped his teeth together and stared at him. "It's none of your business, Pavel. Worry about what you are going to do when we find her."

Pavel nodded. "Sorry."

Oleg pushed away from the table and stood. "We can't use the Tahoe to follow him again. I'll rent two cars. We'll stay in contact with each other by phone. Let's go."

###

Paul pulled the Ford Expedition out of his garage at nine in the morning. He planned to talk with Tatiana before they went to the Department of Motor Vehicles to have her Tennessee license transferred to Florida. It was imperative she not give them any information that may cause security problems.

As he passed the marina a block from his condo, he saw a white Chevrolet sedan pull out of the parking lot. *I don't know ... we'll see.* He made a U-turn. The sedan turned around and followed him as he headed back to his residence. When he reached his driveway, he parked, and walked to the front door.

He pulled out his cell phone, called Miami and Marie transferred him to his boss.

"How you doing today?" Bob asked.

"Good. Did John call you about the security company in Atlanta?"

"Yeah. I just got off the phone with him and was going to call you."

"What did he find out?"

"The company has connections with the Russian mob. John got the information from the FBI and didn't want to tell them why we're interested."

"I thought that might be the case. I don't know what I'm going to do yet, but I'll call you when I make a decision."

"Don't take any chances. The best thing is move her until we figure out what they have up their sleeve."

"You're right. We'll talk later."

When he ended the call he walked upstairs.

Ten minutes later he came out the door carrying a black duffel bag. The Chevy was nowhere in sight. He drove out of the neighborhood. When he stopped for a red light at the intersection of the causeway, he spotted the white car again as it came out of a high rise condo parking lot.

He looked in his rear-view mirror. It had pulled in four cars behind him. "There may be more than one of them." He took a left at the light and drove across the bridge to downtown Clearwater. When he reached North Ft. Harrison Avenue, he turned right. At the third intersection he took a left, drove two blocks and blew through the stop signs as he made the next two consecutive left hand turns back to North Ft. Harrison. He looked in the mirror. The sedan was no longer following him.

He pulled out his cell phone and called Tatiana. Her voice came through the car speakers.

"Hello."

"It's Paul. Pack a bag. We're going to be gone for a few nights."

She didn't reply.

"Did you hear me?"

"Yes." Her voice cracked. "What ... what's wrong?"

"I can't explain now. I'll be there in twenty minutes. When you see me, come out and get in my truck."

"What should I take?"

"Casual clothes and everything you'll need for the next few days ... makeup, toothbrush ... that stuff."

"Why are we—?"

"Please, Tatiana. Do what I say. I'll tell you what happened later."

"Okay. I'll be ready."

"Watch for me ... twenty minutes."

"I will."

Paul hung up and made another call.

"Hampton Inn, Wesley Chapel, how may I help you?"

"Reservations."

"Yes, sir. What day?"

"Today. Two rooms, connecting."

"Please hold."

He continued through residential neighborhoods, staying on two lane streets on his way to Tatiana's.

"Sir, only one set of connecting rooms is available. They're on the third floor."

"I'll take them."

"Your name please."

"Paul D'Angelo. I'll be there in less than two hours."

"We'll hold the rooms until three, Mr. D'Angelo."

"Thank you." Relieved the rooms were available, he ended the call.

A short time later, Paul pulled into the parking lot of Tatiana's apartment complex. He spotted her Mini in front of her door and stopped behind it.

Tatiana ran to his SUV, placed her red carry-on bag on the back seat, and got in next to him. She turned to him with a taut fearful expression. "What's wrong ... what happened?"

"We need to leave Clearwater. We're going to a hotel for a few days."

"Why?"

Paul didn't want to lie to her. He pulled away from the apartment. "Remember when you arrived I told you to be cautious?"

"Yes. I have been."

"I know you have, but I have reason to believe people have come to find you."

She put her hand to her mouth and took a deep breath. "How could that happen?"

He had asked himself the same question. Why were Russians here, and how did they find out she was in Clearwater? He had no proof they were looking for her. If the guy following him had been Middle Eastern or Italian, he'd have Ammar or Santino sitting next to him.

He glanced at her. "Have you contacted anyone since you've been here?"

"No."

"No calls, no texts, no mail?"

She glared at him. "No, I told you. No contact. Nothing. You haven't answered my question. You're not telling me everything are you?"

He pressed his lips together and kept his eyes on the road. *Careful, downplay it. Don't make her panic.* "Someone has been trying to follow me. There's a possibility he could be associated with Russian organized crime."

She froze. "What are we going to do?"

"I contacted the Marshals Service. Hopefully they'll find him and he'll be questioned."

"What about us?"

"I reserved two hotel rooms. We'll stay there a couple of days."

She paused and stared out the window. "Are you sure they found out I'm here and where I live?"

"No. Try not to be concerned. You're not the only protected person with a Russian connection."

"Two nights at the hotel?"

"Two or three."

"Where are we going?"

"Wesley Chapel. It's a town an hour north of Tampa." He turned onto the Causeway and headed toward I-275.

Dmitry sat in a Jeep Wrangler parked near an entrance to the single lane Courtney Campbell Trail on the eastbound side of the causeway. He raised a set of binoculars to watch vehicles approaching from Clearwater.

When Oleg had suggested they watch the roads leading to Tampa, he thought his boss was crazy. The chances of seeing the car the Marshal was driving were slim. His body stiffened, and he leaned forward as a red front license plate came into view. He focused on the vehicle waiting for it to get closer, then he smiled. *Just as Oleg described it, a silver Ford, and a red Boston Strong front license plate.*

He slammed the Jeep into drive and pulled onto the causeway.

CHAPTER XIV

REVELATIONS

Paul stayed on major highways and kept checking the traffic behind him as he drove to the hotel. During their hour-long drive, he steered the conversation away from the possible danger Tatiana was in, and toward her years of traveling the world.

After they checked into the Hampton Inn, he called Dan Plummer's cell phone. Without access to a secure line he had to be careful what he said.

"Hi, Paul. What's going on?"

"I'm in a hotel an hour north of Tampa."

"Is she with you?"

"Yeah. Everything falls into place now. They're still following me, and must believe I'll lead them to her. Earlier today I spotted a sedan and decided to take your advice and get her out of town."

"I'll call John and brief him. What name did you use to check-in?"

"My undercover name. I've got connecting rooms."

"You need help? I can put together a security detail and get them there by tonight."

"No. Not yet. Call Mark and tell him to go to my condo ... he has a key. If someone is watching the place, he'll pick up on them."

"Okay. I'll get two guys out of the Tampa Warrant Squad to meet him. Time to rattle cages. What you carrying?"

"My 45, and I brought your play toy with me."

"Good. Any idea how these people found her? Could she have breached her security?"

Paul paused a moment. "For some reason I trust this girl. No. I didn't get the feeling she lied when I asked her if she contacted anyone."

"You sure?"

"I bet my career on it."

"I hope you're right, but think about something. You, Mark, Anjoli, the Branch Chief, the Deputy Chief, and I are the only people that know she was relocated to Tampa. Columbus told me her file is as tight as a rich lady's change

119

purse. John, the Branch Chief, and Anjoli are the only people with access to it."

"I doubt she had anything to do with this."

"Okay. I trust your instinct. I'll call Columbus and brief him. Keep me informed. I'll tell Mark to contact you when he gets to your place. Be safe."

Paul shoved his phone in his pocket and stared at the floor. *Something doesn't add up. I better be right about her.* He took a bottle of water from the mini bar, poured it into a glass, and took a sip.

I need to be prepared. He walked across the room, picked up his duffel bag and set it on the bed. Once unzipped, he removed the HK MP7 and a forty round magazine. He inserted the magazine into the weapon, jacked a round into the chamber, and flipped the switch to the safe position. Before he returned it to his bag, he checked the shoulder sling.

Paul opened the connecting door leading to Tatiana's room and knocked.

It swung open and Tatiana stood there staring at him. "I'm scared. What are we going to do? Why are people trying to find me? Is Anton still in jail?"

"One question at a time." He took her hand and guided her to a small table in his room. "Do you know what Anton did for the Russian mob?

"No. He carried a gun, but everyone in Russia who works for a security service does. After I came into your program, I learned more."

"Did Anton tell you?"

"No. I asked Mark to be honest with me ... he told me. I couldn't believe it. Do you know Anton had three million dollars?"

"No one mentioned that much money."

She raised her eyebrows.

"Where did he get it?"

"Anton said he saved for many years."

Paul's index finger moved from side to side on the table while he looked at her. "If he put $10,000 in the bank each month, it would take over twenty years to save that much."

She lowered her head, stood, and walked to the window. Her shoulders were back, and hips swayed from side to side. His eyes locked on her rhythmic movement. The word *sexy* bounced around in his head.

When she turned and walked back to the table, tears filled her eyes.

Radiant and intoxicating ... even when she's upset. He took a deep breath and motioned to the chair.

She picked up a napkin, dabbed her eyes and sat. "I'm sorry. I haven't been completely honest with you. It's easy to hide three million dollars in diamonds."

He paused and folded his hands in front of him. *I'm in deep shit if she's been setting me up.* "So that's why you and Anton went to Amsterdam?"

"Yes."

"Did he tell you where he hid them?"

She hesitated. "He didn't hide them."

He sat up straight "Okay. Let's go back over this. Anton had millions of dollars in diamonds?"

"Yes, Three million, but they're worth much more now."

"More than what he paid?"

"Yes. He paid broker prices."

"What's their retail value?"

"Five million or more."

Paul shook his head "And he bought them with his own money?"

"That's what he said."

"Did Anton say what he did with them?"

"They're safe."

Anger welled up in his body. For the first time since he met her, he was pissed. He leaned across the table and glared into her eyes. "Lie to me, Tatiana, and with one phone call I'll arrange for you to be moved to a hotel in Miami. Someone else will deal with you."

A look of terror came across her face. Her hands shook. "I've never really lied to you. I've hidden things by not telling you exactly what happened. The diamonds are in my safe deposit box."

His mouth dropped open. "All of them?"

She closed her eyes and nodded.

Holy shit! Paul rubbed his temples. "Did Anton give them to you?"

"Yes, to hold."

"They don't belong to you."

"They do now."

He lowered his voice. "If, as you said, you're finished with him, what are you going to do when he gets out of prison and wants them back?"

123

"You're helping me create a new identity. Why give them to him? He'll never find me."

Paul pushed his chair away from the table. "I need a stronger drink." He walked to the minibar.

"Please get me a wine."

He grabbed a bottle of orange juice, white wine, and two glasses.

Tatiana took the wine and filled her glass.

Paul sat and stared into her eyes. "When he gets out of prison, he'll ask for them. They are his."

"Who will he ask? He doesn't want the U.S. Government to find out he has them."

"Did he steal the three million?"

She shrugged. "If he did, someone would have reported it. Have you heard anything?"

He rubbed the back of his neck. *She's right. There's nothing in any of the files about missing money.*

Dmitry sat in the Jeep at the Holiday Inn Express & Suites, directly across from the Hampton Inn. He tapped his cell phone screen and turned on the speaker.

"Yes," Oleg said.

"I followed him. He and a girl are staying at a Hampton Inn, one hour north of Tampa."

"Is it the ballerina?"

"I don't know."

"Did you get their room number?"

"Not yet, but I have a plan."

CHAPTER XV

SO MUCH FOR PLANS

Paul and Tatiana sat at the table in his hotel room. An empty pizza box lay on a chair. A bottle of red wine, and a bottle of water, stood in the center of the table. They both had half-full glasses in front of them.

Tatiana took a sip of wine and stared at him. "What are we going to do?"

"Like I said. We'll spend a couple of nights here. U.S. Marshals from Tampa, and men from Witness Security, are looking for the guy that was following me. When he's found, he'll be questioned."

"I mean us. Are we supposed to sit around and wait?"

"Tomorrow we can go out for a while ... maybe lunch."

Paul refilled her glass of wine. It would be easy for her to claim he made advances. Accommodating a witness and placing his job in jeopardy wasn't something he normally did. But Tatiana was not your typical witness, she was an innocent pawn caught up in an international crime investigation. Had her boyfriend not insisted she be brought into the program, she wouldn't be in this situation. "Why did you decide to come into the Witness Security Program?"

Tatiana shrugged. "I didn't want to. Anton told me I'd never be safe unless I did."

Paul nodded. "He might have been right. You may not have knowledge of his criminal activities, but if his former associates threaten you, he might decide to quit testifying."

"That won't happen. His friends are fools if they believe he'll do anything that would mean more time in jail. Once they realize he doesn't care what happens to Tatiana Fedorka, they won't harm me."

"I hope you're right, but it looks as if they're certain you are their salvation."

"I don't think so. Anton told me he worked with many people in the Russian government and said they are cautious. They're not going to hurt an American citizen."

Paul raised a finger. "That's a chance I can't take. You're my responsibility."

She reached across the table and squeezed his hand. "Thank you. I know I'm safe while you're with me."

He didn't pull his hand from hers and waited for her to sit back. "It's late. You better go to bed. Make sure you keep everything packed. I want you to be prepared if we need to get out of here fast."

"I don't want to stay in my room alone."

"We'll keep the doors between the rooms open. You'll be safe."

Oleg, Pavel, and Dmitry sat in the jeep at the Holiday Inn Express & Suites parking lot at four in the morning.

Dmitry handed Oleg a key card. "They have connecting rooms. This will open her door."

Oleg smiled. "How much did it cost?"

"Four hundred dollars."

"In Moscow we could have gotten it for fifty," Pavel said.

Oleg stared at him. "We're not in Moscow, Pavel. Things cost more here. We can't even threaten anyone with a trip to a labor camp in Siberia. We'll go in an hour. I'll wait in the Jeep. Make sure it's the ballerina. If it is, grab her and bring her out the side entrance."

Paul dozed on the couch, fully clothed. His Glock 45 sat within reach on the coffee table. His eyes opened at the sound of a moan and glanced at the connecting doors. The one on her side was almost closed. *I left that open. I guess I was snoring, and she closed it.* He shut his eyes.

The unmistakable click of a door latch brought him to his feet. He grabbed his pistol and bolted into Tatiana's room.

A bed sheet lay strewn across the floor, and a chair was tipped over in the middle of the room. Tatiana was gone. He rushed into the corridor.

Two men, holding Tatiana by the arms, were dragging her toward the stairwell.

"Stop! Let her go!"

Tatiana, still in her pajamas, turned her head to look at him. Duct tape covered her mouth and her eyes were wide with terror.

One of the men released her, pulled a pistol from his waistband and swung it toward him.

Adrenalin shot through his body. Paul dropped to one knee and fired twice the instant he saw a muzzle flash. He cringed at a sharp pain in his left side as he watched the guy fall backwards from the impact of the .45 caliber hollow-point bullets. The second man shoved Tatiana to the floor and bolted through the stairwell door.

Tatiana pulled the tape from her mouth and screamed. She looked at the man bleeding on the floor next to her and scrambled on her hands and knees towards Paul.

Paul glanced at his blood-stained shirt, raised it, and saw a grazing wound below his ribs. Blood trickled to his waistline. He placed his hand over his heart, stiffened and took a deep breath. The speed and strength of its beat made him pause and not move.

Tatiana had crawled halfway to him when he stood, rushed to her, and pulled her from the floor. "Quick. We need to get our bags and leave."

He followed her to the room and pulled the key card from his pocket. *Stay calm, don't do anything to make her panic and lose control.*

As he entered, the door across the hall opened. A young man in his underwear stuck his head into the hallway.

Paul looked at him. "Did you hear a gun shot?"

The man stared at him without blinking. "It was a loud bang, then someone screamed. What happened?"

"I don't know." He pointed down the hall. "A guy is on the floor bleeding. We better keep our doors closed." He stepped inside, slammed the door.

Tatiana clutched at him and sank into his arms. She sobbed and buried her face against his chest. When she released him, she dropped to the floor and looked up. Her face contorted and eyes filled with tears. "You've been shot!" She leapt to her feet. "Let me see it." She reached for his shirt.

He held up a hand. "It's not bad ... a little flesh wound. Please hurry. We need to get our bags and get out of here before the police arrive."

"Why? Will they arrest us?"

"No, but I don't want to wait around to explain what happened."

She stripped off her pajamas and stood in the middle of the room with a terrified expression on her face. Wearing only red panties, she scrambled to pull on a pair of jeans. His mouth dropped open.

She stopped, looked at him, and placed her hands over her bare breasts.

Everything is turning to shit. I shouldn't be here alone with her. She's frightened to death. He forced a smile. "Hurry and don't forget your shirt." He headed to his room.

Oleg sat behind the wheel of the Jeep parked in front of a side entrance to the hotel.

Dmitry bolted from a door and jumped into the passenger seat.

Oleg raised both his hands. "Where's Pavel and the girl?"

"The Marshal woke up. Pavel was stupid and pulled his pistol. The guy shot him. He may be dead."

Oleg slammed the Wrangler into gear and sped toward the exit road.

CHAPTER XVI

SAFETY

After Paul and Tatiana both had their bags packed and ready to go, he opened the door and checked the hallway. He reached back and took her hand. They stepped from the room and glanced at the body lying at the end of the hall. He pulled her in the opposite direction. "We'll go down the stairs at the other end." They ran to the second stairway, raced to ground level, and left the hotel through a side entrance.

When they reached his SUV, he threw their bags into the back seat and they jumped in.

Paul backed out of the parking space, drove from the hotel parking lot, and turned right onto State Road 56.

Tatiana grabbed his arm. "Where are we going?"

"To the Sheriff's District Office. It's a twenty-minute drive from here. You'll be safe there."

She tightened her grip on his arm. "Please don't leave me."

He glanced at her. "That's not going to happen. I'll never leave you. My job is to keep you safe. I plan to make sure you are. Get my duffel bag from the back seat. Set it on the console between us."

She turned around, grabbed the bag and returned to her seat.

"Unzip it for me."

"What's in it?" She pulled the zipper.

"My insurance policy." Paul removed the HK MP7, flipped the fire selector switch to full automatic, and set it on his lap.

She gasped. "What kind of gun is that?"

"The Germans call it a machine pistol."

"It's so small."

"Small but deadly."

Two police cars, with their emergency lights flashing, passed them going in the opposite direction. Thirty seconds later a black Jeep pulled beside him and matched his speed. The passenger lowered his window and waved for him to pull to the side of the road.

He ignored the man.

The jeep eased closer.

When it came within two feet of his Ford, Tatiana looked at the guy sitting in the passenger seat. She pointed and screamed. "That's one of the men who tried to take me!"

Paul lowered his window, raised the MP7, and pointed it at the man.

Tires screeched and smoke bellowed from under the Jeep as it skidded to a stop.

Paul slammed his foot against the accelerator and sped toward the traffic light one hundred yards in front of him. He ran the red light as he turned left onto Trinity Boulevard. A minute later he pulled into the parking lot of the Sheriff's Trinity Division office. He stopped in the no parking zone in front of the entrance.

Paul shoved the selector switch to the safe position and placed the MP7 back into the duffel bag. He zipped it closed and picked it up. "While we're here, they'll ask many questions. Don't mention the Witness Security Program. I'm going to tell them you're helping me find a fugitive."

"I won't."

"Good. Leave your bag here."

They jumped from the SUV and went inside the Sheriff's Office.

A uniformed officer sat at a desk behind a glass enclosure.

The Deputy Sheriff stood and pointed at Paul. "You can't park there," he motioned with his thumb extended, "Move it."

Paul flipped opened his credential case and placed it flat against the glass. "I'm U.S. Marshal Inspector Paul Baldini. This is an emergency. You just had a shooting reported at the Hampton Inn on I-275. The dead guy on the third floor tried to kill me."

The deputy, his mouth hanging open, stared at the blood on Paul's shirt. "You're bleeding."

Paul removed his credentials from the glass. "I need to see the person who is in charge. Is there a paramedic at the fire station next door?"

"Yes, sir."

"Please call and get him over here so he can bandage me up."

The deputy pointed at a door. "I'll let you in and call the lieutenant. Wait in that room."

Paul opened the door when he heard it unlock. He and Tatiana walked into an unoccupied room with two rows of chairs in front of a desk.

A door opened and a lieutenant in uniform walked in. "May I see your identification?"

Paul opened his credential case and held it up.

The lieutenant studied the two cards in the open case. "I'm Lieutenant Ron Walker." He held out his hand.

"Inspector Paul Baldini, nice to meet you." He motioned to Tatiana. "This is Ms. Demko."

Walker nodded to Tatiana and looked at Paul. "She your partner?"

Tatiana's security had been breached, but he had no reason to tell anyone, including the local police, or any other law enforcement officer, that she was a protected witness. "No. She's helping the Marshals Service locate a fugitive."

Walker smiled at Tatiana. "Thank you for assisting law enforcement."

She nodded.

He turned to Paul. "How bad are you hurt?"

"Just a grazing wound."

"A paramedic is on his way. Are you armed?"

Paul nodded.

"Come with me. There's a gun locker you can use on your way to my office."

They followed the lieutenant through a door and into a hallway.

Walker looked at Paul and pointed to a standing gun locker against a wall. "Put your weapon in there."

Paul opened one of the small doors, unloaded his Glock 45, slid it into the opening, and locked the door. He looked at Walker and raised his eyebrows. "The other one won't fit."

"What else do you have?"

He opened his duffel, pulled out the MP7, and removed the magazine and the chambered round.

Walker furrowed his brow. His eyes moved between the weapon and Paul. "Jesus! You carry that all the time?"

"No, only on special occasions."

The Lieutenant smiled. "I don't want any of my men to see it. Rumors will start flying around here, and then next week they'll each want one. As long as it's unloaded put it back in your bag."

While an EMT bandaged his flesh wound, Paul spent the next thirty minutes recounting to Lt. Walker what had happened at the hotel.

He skipped over the details about Tatiana being a protected witness. He portrayed her as someone who had information on a federal fugitive's whereabouts in Tampa.

She sat patiently listening to him.

"Ms. Demko could have been in danger if she stayed overnight in Tampa. That's something I couldn't live with so I brought her up here for the night. Somehow associates of the fugitive found us, and two men tried to kidnap her."

Walker frowned, "How'd they get into her room?"

"The fugitive is a known Russian organized crime figure. Money is no problem. They could have paid off the night clerk and gotten a keycard."

"The manager at the hotel is a friend of mine." Walker raised his eyebrows and smiled. "We'll find out what happened."

"When they grabbed her, I heard the door latch to her room click, ran into the hall, and saw them dragging her to the stairwell. One of them pulled a pistol. I put two 45 caliber rounds in him at the same time he fired at me. I was lucky, he wasn't."

"What was he carrying?" Walker asked.

Paul shook his head. "Not sure, but it resembled a Browing Hi-Power."

Walker paused, glanced at the floor, and looked back at him. "The gun is must be near the body, and the bullet somewhere in the hallway wall."

"I wanted to get to the nearest Sheriff's office as soon as possible so we drove here. On our way, a black Jeep pulled alongside us. I'm not familiar with the different models, but it had typical Wrangler fenders, four doors and a hardtop."

Walker frowned. "Where?"

"On State Road 54, less than a quarter mile east of the Trinity Boulevard traffic light. Ms. Demko recognized the guy in the passenger's seat. Counting the guy lying in the hotel hallway, there must have been three of them. I stuck the MP7 out the window, and they locked their brakes."

Walker grinned. "I don't blame them. You get a plate number?"

"No, never saw the back bumper."

Walker got up from behind his desk. "Wait here. I need to call the Sheriff and tell him what you told me. I'll get the description of the Jeep sent out to our patrol units."

Paul stood. "One other thing. I don't want Ms. Demko's name in any of the reports."

"No problem, we'll list her as a confidential informant."

Paul held out the keys to his SUV. "In case you want to have someone move my vehicle."

"I'm not worried. I'll tell the deputy up front it's not to be moved."

"Thank you. I'm going to make a call and get a few of my men here. Then we can leave and let your guys do their job."

"We'll find the bastards," Walker said on his way out of the office.

When they were alone, Tatiana turned to him. "What's going to happen to me?"

He slid his chair in front of hers and leaned forward.

"I don't know yet. The guys at the hotel, and whoever they are working for, know you're in Tampa. That's a security breach." *She's going to be moved, but I don't want to be the one who hits her with bad news.* "There's a possibility headquarters will want to move you to another city. That could mean another name change."

Tatiana stared at him and shook her head. "I'm not leaving Clearwater, and I don't want anyone except you to help me. My name has been changed twice. I've been moved to two different cities. I can't keep doing this."

Paul looked into her eyes and took a deep breath. "Your case is not typical. Criminals come into the program because they want something in return for their testimony. They're facing a difficult decision. Do I live, or take my chances and maybe die? You're here because someone else wants you here. When you came into the program the inspector that interviewed you should have told you Witness Security is a program of last resort."

Tatiana leaned toward him. "Do you want me here?"

He hesitated and smiled. "What I want doesn't matter."

"Yes, it does. It matters to me."

"And what happens to you matters to me. It's my job."

She jumped out of her chair. "The hell with your job. I need help. I want to be happy. This is not how I want to live." Her eyes widened, and she lowered her head. When she looked back at him her expression had relaxed. "I'm sorry I raised my voice."

"Are you happy in Clearwater?"

"Yes. You've been wonderful to me ... you're strong and have a positive attitude. I have a future here."

"If you're adamant about staying, you may have to voluntarily leave the program."

"If I'm forced to, I'll leave. I did nothing illegal. I don't know everything Anton did, or the people he worked for."

"I understand, but please think it over before you make a decision. I'll see what I can do. Entering the Witness Security Program is the most difficult thing a person can face.

She nodded.

"You gave up everything; your past; your name, your family, friends, and your background. Then you started over as a different person, in a place you've never been. The mental anguish takes its toll. Let's wait and see what happens."

She nodded. "Okay, but I don't think I can go on without you."

"You're important to me, Tatiana. But I'm not the only Witness Security Specialist on earth."

"I understand that, but you are the one I want."

And I'd like you to stay. Paul smiled. "And I wish every witness was as nice as you. We'll discuss it later. I need to make a few calls." He pulled out his phone and walked across the room.

Mark answered on the second ring. "Paul, where the hell are you?"

"At the Pasco County Sheriff's Trinity Division Office. It's off of State Road 54. Are you at my place?"

"Yeah, with three guys from the Tampa Warrant Squad. Hold on a second."

Mark's muffled words filled the background.

"You still there?"

"Yes," Paul said.

"The Tampa guys know where you are."

"Good. Come here as quick as you can. I need to get this young lady to a safe place."

"Your boss said you were at a hotel. What are you doing at the sheriff's office?"

"Long story. The Russians found us. One of them is dead, and I have a gunshot wound on my side. An EMT patched it up. I've got to find a new place to hide our girl."

"Christ. That's the second time you've been shot. You okay?"

"Yeah. This isn't as bad as the last one."

"You tell Plummer yet?"

"No. I'll call him next."

"Okay. We're on our way."

Paul ended the call and tapped the screen of his phone.

Bob answered. "Everything okay?"

"Now it is. Mark and guys from Tampa are on their way to meet me."

"What happened?"

He told his boss everything.

CHAPTER XVII

THE ARREST

The next day, Paul walked into a suite at the Sailport Hotel on Tampa's west side.

Mark and Tatiana sat in the living room.

"Finished?" Mark asked.

"Yeah. They put in a few stitches and told me to come back in ten days."

Paul looked at Tatiana. "We'll be here until we can decide it's safe for you in Clearwater, or WITSEC Headquarters makes a decision to move you."

She sat up. "If they tell me I must go, I'll voluntarily leave the program."

Mark raised his hand. "We'll wait to see. You never know. The chances are that they'll say you have to move, but let's wait for them to make a decision."

Paul's cell phone beeped, and he checked the text message. "Mark and I have to call our Miami office. Relax, we'll be back in a half hour."

Tatiana nodded.

They walked out, nodded to an inspector guarding the door, and entered the suite across the hall. Both sat at a round table near the small kitchen.

"Does Plummer want to talk to us?"

"No. That was from the Sheriff's Office. They picked up the two guys in the Jeep. Both are in the Pasco County jail. Weapons charges and attempted kidnapping. Lieutenant Walker asked me to call him. When I finish, I'll call Miami. We'll have Bob get the FBI involved. I want the case to get into the hands of the U.S. Attorney so the locals can drop everything."

"Good idea."

"One other thing. I saw the same doctor that took care of the gunshot wound to my back. There's a problem."

Mark frowned. "The bullet that's still in you?"

Paul pressed his lips together and nodded. "The trauma from the bullet to my side caused it to move closer to my spine."

"Close enough to be dangerous?"

"Could be. He wants to do a CT scan."

###

Victor sat at his desk and stared at his cell phone. He picked it up, tapped the screen, and read the text message.

`There is a problem with our men in Tampa.`

He had informed Oleg that Tatiana might be in Tampa, but that was only a hunch based on what had been written on a piece of paper. *Who went to Tampa, and why aren't they telling me what kind of problem they got themselves into?* The computer keyboard on his desk caught his eye. He pulled it in front of him and typed Faina Lobanov. The search took him to Tatiana Fedorka's file. *Dammit. If she's still on the program where is her active file?* He pushed away from his desk and walked to Anjoli's cubical.

"How are you today, Anjoli?"

"Fine. What can I do for you?"

"I read a *New York Times* article about a trial one of our witnesses will be testifying in. I guess it's a big case."

She tilted her head. "Who?"

"A guy named Anton Novikoff ... he's a prisoner witness."

"Where's the trial being held?"

"Manhattan."

"That's the Southern District Court. Richard is the Case Manager for that area. I've got enough to do. If it's not in my region, I don't worry about it. You could check with him, or call the guys at New York Metro. Why are you interested in a New York case?"

Victor shrugged. "I'm not. I read the article and wondered how the news media got the name of one of our witnesses?"

"I'll bet the U.S. Attorney's office gave it to them. Everyone wants publicity."

He nodded. "Yeah, but doesn't that make it harder for the guys on the protection detail to get the witness safely in and out of the courthouse?"

She looked at him and smiled. "The Inspectors working in the field are good at what they do. I'm sure you worked court cases in Pittsburgh. Each office has their ways."

"Actually I was briefly assigned to a couple of relocated witness cases ... never had the opportunity to work a court production."

Anjoli frowned. "They taught it in WITSEC Basic, didn't they?"

"Yeah, but we were told the detail supervisor would come up with a plan and brief everyone working the detail."

"The next time a witness is going to testify in our region, we'll arrange for you to work the detail for a few days. Miami has a drug trial coming up in the next month or so."

Victor nodded and smiled. "Good idea, thank you." He returned to his desk.

Two days later, John Colombus sat in his office with Chief Inspector Sam Brooks from the International Investigations Branch. He handed Sam a folder. "This report was put together by Lester Young from IT. We've got enough on Victor to put him away for a long time. Before his security clearance was upgraded, he made five attempts to access top secret cases. Once it was upgraded to TS, he actively tried to locate Tatiana Fedorka."

Sam scanned through the report. "With the information in the report, and the cell phone records we have, this guy is toast."

John nodded. "Where are the FBI Agents?"

"Down stairs ... just outside the front door. Victor is our problem, and this is our territory."

"Good. I didn't want them stepping foot into the WITSEC Division. You want to do the honors?"

Sam smiled. "I'd love to. Think he'll be a problem?"

"No. He'll be so surprised he'll freeze. I'll call and tell him to come up here."

He picked up the phone and dialed. "Victor, ... John Colombus, come to my office, we need to speak."

The two men stood in the center of the room and waited.

Victor knocked on the doorframe and entered.

John introduced him to Sam and took a step back.

Victor extended his hand.

Sam stared at the young case manager and shook his head. "Inspector Serban, you're under arrest." He pulled a set of handcuffs from his waistband. "Turn around and place your hands behind your back."

Victor's eyes widened and his face turned ashen. "What did—"

John stepped behind him.

"Don't talk," Sam said. "Do as I say. Turn around and place your hands behind your back."

Victor turned and sucked in air when his eyes met those of the Deputy Chief. His legs gave out, and he dropped to his knees.

After Victor had been turned over to the FBI, John entered Anjoli's cubicle. "It's a sad day for the U.S. Marshals Service. We need to discuss Tatiana's case."

Anjoli shook her head. "I feel sorry for her. Paul and I talked. Her only mistake was getting involved with Anton Novikoff."

He raised his eyebrows and nodded. "I know."

"Paul said she wrote Anton a letter and ended their relationship. What are we going to do with her?"

"Not much choice," he shrugged, "she has to be moved."

"She's been through hell. Isn't there a way to allow her to stay in Paul's area?"

"Actually, Anjoli, she may no longer be in danger, but we can't take a chance. We need to follow the rules." He stood. "Call Paul and have him break the news to her."

"Have you read his last report, Chief?"

"No, why?"

"If she's told to move, she said she will voluntarily terminate."

"Someone has to be the hard-ass. Tell Paul to take the form with him. She can sign it." He took one step and stopped. "Keep this to yourself. I'm working on something that may guarantee her safety. If it works out, we may be able to revisit the case and help her later."

"Have you told Paul?"

"The Chief of WITSEC, the Director," he tapped his chest with his thumb, "and I are working on it. Don't say anything to Paul. I'll find out more the day after tomorrow."

"Okay. I'll call him."

After John had left, Anjoli scrolled through the contacts list on her cell phone and tapped the screen.

Paul answered. "Yes."

"You starting to answer the phone like I do?"

"Only when you call, Anjoli."

"I called your cell because I didn't think you'd be in the office."

"I'm not."

"I received her passport yesterday. I'm going to overnight it to you."

"No need to hurry."

"You said she may leave the program, and I want to get it to her as soon as possible. I spoke with the Deputy Chief. He said she needs to be relocated."

"Then I'm sure she'll leave."

"Wish she wouldn't, but don't say anything to her yet. I'm going to type up the voluntary termination form with her name on it. I'll mail it to you in a day or so."

Paul hesitated. "Mail? Send me a copy on the secure system."

"No. I want it to go in the mail."

"Okay, Anjoli. What the hell's going on? Did Colombus put the cuffs on Victor yet?"

"You heard about that?"

"Of course. I'm the one who got shot."

"They took him out of here an hour ago."

"So, why send me a personalized termination form by snail mail?"

"I can't tell you."

"What do you mean you can't tell me?"

"Do you trust me?"

"Come on, Anjoli, you know I do."

"Then wait for the mail. It will take about five working days to get there."

"Slip me a hint."

"I can't. I made a promise. And before you take the form to her, call me. I may have more information."

"You're a hard-ass Anj."

"No. Colombus is. He made the decision to move her."

"She's apprehensive about what may happen. I wish we could do something for her."

"That's why I'm overnighting the passport. Who knows how things will turn out?"

"Sounds as if someone has something up their sleeve. Is it good?"

"I wasn't told much, but it may be. That's all I can say. How's your side?"

"Another week and the stitches will be removed. I'll patiently wait for the form to arrive. Give me a call if you hear more."

"I will. Talk to you later."

CHAPTER XVIII

THE DEAL

A week after he made the decision to relocate Tatiana, John Colombus walked into the outer office of the Secretary of State. The plan he come up with would work if presented in the right way. The fact that the Secretary had arranged a meeting meant he liked the idea.

A woman behind a desk looked up at him. "May I help you, sir?"

"I'm U.S. Marshals Service Deputy Chief John Colombus. I have an appointment with the Secretary."

She motioned to a leather couch. "He's expecting you. I'll inform him you're here."

John sat and set the folder he was carrying on a short circular table next to the chair. He looked around the well-furnished office. On each side of the polished wooden desk, matching wood boxes held a stack of folders. Beside the desk sat a matching three cabinet credenza. Above it hung a large oil painting of a ship passing the Statue of Liberty.

The woman stood. "He'll see you now." She led him across the room and opened a door.

John walked into Harrison Lambert's opulent office. Secretary Lambert stood behind an oak executive desk. The seal of the Department of State was carved into its front panel. Behind him wood bookcases stood above matching cabinet drawers. The shelves were packed with books.

Lambert walked from behind his desk. "Nice to meet you, Chief Colombus." He extended his hand.

"It's my pleasure, sir."

Lambert motioned to two burgundy leather armchairs in front of a coffee table and sat on a matching leather couch against a wall. "Our guest will be here any moment. Security called. They're bringing him up now."

John handed him the folder. "Copies of the arrest reports, the FBI Form 302, as well as photos of the men arrested and the man that is dead. I was told you received the background information the CIA completed on each of the men."

"I did. I plan to focus on Oleg Vasilev, the GRU Agent. The dead one we won't worry about, and the other guy is nothing, but a hired thug. Have you met the Ambassador?"

"No, sir."

"He's a reasonable old-timer. Hopefully he'll see things our way."

There was a knock on the door and it opened.

Russian Ambassador Leonid Minsky stepped in and walked to Lambert. He held out his hand and spoke with an accent. "Good morning, Mr. Secretary. I trust everything is well."

"I'm sure it will be after our meeting." He motioned to John. "Please let me introduce Chief John Colombus. He has operational responsibility for the U.S. Department of Justice's Witness Security Program."

Minsky shook John's hand. "My pleasure, Mr. Colombus. We have a similar program in Russia."

John nodded. *I know. We gave you our organizational chart and helped you create it.* "Nice to meet you, Mr. Ambassador."

Lambert waved toward the chairs across from the couch.

John and Minsky took chairs. Lambert sat on the couch and picked up the folder beside him. He rubbed his chin and looked at Minsky. "There's something you can help me with.

Minsky smiled. "Of course. Russia is always open to mutual aid."

"Sadly, three Russian nationals committed a crime, and two of them are in jail in Florida."

Minsky nodded. "The police representative at our embassy mentioned it to me. Both our countries have criminals."

Lambert removed a photo from the folder and handed it to him. "This is Pavel Gurkin. The poor man is dead." He handed the Ambassador a second photo. "Dmitry Dobrow. He has ties to organized crime and is being held by the police." The third photo he held up. "This is Oleg Vasilev. He's the one I would like to focus on." He handed Minsky the picture.

The Russian glanced at the photos and stopped on Oleg's picture. "If they committed a crime, they must face justice in your country."

"They will, but Chief Colombus has proposed something to me. With your help, we may be able to agree upon the proposal, and carry out his plan."

Minsky hesitated, glanced at John, and turned to Lambert. "I do not see how my government can help."

Lambert raised his eyebrows. "Pavel was killed during the commission of a kidnapping, and the three men tried to kill a United States Marshal. The two in custody will probably spend the rest of their lives in a federal prison. Should the charges be upgraded to a capital offense, Oleg Vasilev, and Dmitry, may be facing the death penalty."

Minsky shrugged.

Lambert turned to John. "Chief Colombus, please explain your proposal to the ambassador."

John leaned forward. "Sir. The men were caught attempting to kidnap a US and Ukrainian citizen named Tatiana Fedorka, and kill a Witness Security Inspector, one of my investigators. We know Oleg Vasilev is an agent of the GRU. For that reason his activities in Florida must have been known and sanctioned by someone in the Russian government. We've had many discussions with him. We plan to offer him the services of our Witness Security Program, and the chance of a new life in America. All we ask in return is that he agree to testify in cases developed in the future." He waited for a reaction. There was none.

Minsky turned to Lambert. "What is the proposal?"

John glanced at Lambert, and before he continued, waited for a nod. "Ms. Fedorka was once the girlfriend of a man named Anton Novikoff, a Russian mob associate. She has since cut all ties with him, knows nothing of his activities, and is not scheduled to testify in any court." He looked at Lambert.

"Leonid, we want assurances that Ms. Fedorka is safe to live in the United States without fear of being accosted by Russian agents or mobsters. If someone in your government can arrange that, the United States Attorney for the Middle District of Florida will drop the charges. We would be open to putting Oleg and his friend Dmitry on a plane to Moscow."

Minsky sighed. "I cannot speak for every Russian citizen."

Lambert leaned forward. "Understandable. But I'm sure that the words of the Russian Ambassador to the United States of America carry a lot of weight. Should word go out to the right people, Ms. Fedorka will have nothing to fear. Then our governments can continue with more pressing matters such as trade agreements and cooperation on international terrorism. Without Moscow's approval, and with the information Oleg Vasilev may offer us, I hate to think how difficult it will be to continue talks on a number of issues important to our countries."

Minsky smiled. "Moscow will welcome your proposal."

"One more thing," said Lambert. "Should Ms. Fedorka have an unfortunate accident, you and I may see a need to revisit this issue."

Minsky laughed. "Hopefully she is in good shape, and not prone to accidents. I think she will be fine."

Lambert stood. "Thank you for your cooperation Mr. Ambassador. The next time I see Mr. Putin I'll tell him how much of a pleasure it is to work with you." He handed the ambassador a business card. "This is Chief Colombus' card. A member of your staff can contact him and arrangements will be made to place Oleg and Dmitry on a flight bound for Moscow."

Minsky took the card and shook John's hand. "I'll tell one of my aides to call you." He turned to Lambert. "May I ask for the other man's body to be sent to Russia? I'm sure his family will want to bury him in the motherland."

"I'll make the arrangements and provide your aide with the details." John said.

Minsky nodded to both men and left the office.

Lambert walked John to the door. "Thank you for your valuable assistance. If I need anything further may I call you?"

"Please do."

###

John got off the elevator at Marshals Service Headquarters and headed to the Witness Security Division. As he approached the door, it flew open, and two men he did not recognize rushed past him.

When he entered the office, Anjoli, with a worried look on her face, scurried to him. "We've been trying to call you. Did you get the messages?"

He pulled his cell phone from his pocket. "I turned it off when I was at the State Department." He pressed the power button and glanced at the office staff standing across the room. "Why is everyone staring? What the hell is going on?"

Anjoli moved close to him. "You haven't heard?"

"What?"

"Victor hanged himself at the Central Detention Facility. They found him an hour ago. He's dead."

He tightened his jaw and nodded. "Who's handling it?"

"The enforcement side of the house."

"I'll be in my office." He shook his head and walked away.

When he reached his desk, he called the Miami Metro office. As soon as Marie answered he cut her off. "Marie, John Colombus. Tell Bob I need to talk to him."

"Yes, Sir."

"Hi, John. What's going on?"

"Call Paul. Tell him I'm coming to visit the day after tomorrow."

"Is everything okay?"

"Some good news, some bad."

"What's the good?"

"The girl may not need to be relocated. Don't say anything, I want to tell him."

"The bad?"

"Victor Serban hanged himself in his cell."

"Did they get to him in time?"

"No."

"Shit. It would have been nice to find out how they turned him."

"Doesn't matter now. The day after tomorrow I'll take an early flight to Tampa. I want you to meet me at the airport. We'll both go to his office."

"I'll drive over tomorrow evening."

"Good. I'll call you with my itinerary. Talk to you later." John ended the call.

Bob called Paul. "You busy?"

Paul chuckled. "I'm always busy when the boss calls."

"You hear about Victor yet?"

"Yeah, good news travels fast."

"I'm driving over tomorrow night. I'll pick up Colombus at the airport the next morning and we're coming to your office."

"Want me to meet you tomorrow?"

"No. I'm not sure when I'll get to Tampa."

"Good. I was going to ask to meet with you so we can discuss the Tampa cases."

"We'll talk about things when John and I get there. I'll let you know when we're on our way."

"I'll be in the office early. See you then."

Tatiana was sick of The Sailport Hotel and living out of a suitcase. The marshals assigned to protect her were courteous, but aloof and reserved.

Paul knocked on the door and entered. The moment the door closed she threw her arms around him

"Any news about me being moved?" she asked.

He took her hand, and they walked to the couch. "No, but there will be the day after tomorrow. My boss and the Deputy Chief of WITSEC are coming to my office."

He had no intention of telling her agency business and what Victor Serban had done. His outlook on life had changed since she arrived. In the past week they had spent hours sitting in the suite discussing what had happened the night he had taken a bullet in the side for her. *Who the hell was it that said life's a bitch and then you die?*

"Once I speak to them, everything will be okay."

CHAPTER XIX

SHE'S SAFE

The next morning, John, Bob and Paul sat in Paul's office exchanging small talk.

"How's your side?" John asked.

"Not bad ... a few stitches."

"If you need time off, take it."

"I'm okay. Things should get back to normal now."

"Hopefully." John said. "What ever happened to the lawsuit you filed against the airline?"

"Once the NTSB determined it was pilot error they settled."

Bob furrowed his brow. "Were you satisfied with the outcome?"

Paul pressed his lips together. "I lost my wife. It's been a difficult five years. Celeste meant the world to me. As for the settlement, I collected much more than I'll ever make working for the government the rest of my life. That doesn't make it any less painful." He glanced at John. "Why the visit to Tampa?"

"A couple of days ago I spent time with the Secretary of State. We had a productive discussion with Leonid Minsky, the Russian ambassador. The U.S. Attorney's office is going to drop the charges against the two Russians."

Paul bolted upright. "One of them tried to kill me."

John held up his hand. "Yes, but it's in our best interest to make sure Ms. Fedorka remains safe, and doesn't have to look over her shoulder for the rest of her life."

"What kind of deal did you make?" Paul asked.

"Minsky assured us the right people would be told to back off."

Bob frowned. "You believe him?"

"The Secretary of State told him relations between the US and Russia depended on it. He also told him the girl knew nothing about her boyfriend's crimes and is not testifying in any cases."

Paul nodded. "Since the day she arrived, that's what she's said."

"Anton Novikoff." John said. "Another wrench has been thrown into the works. I got a call this morning. A Croatian inmate in the prison unit stabbed him."

"Is he okay?" Bob asked.

"No, he's dead."

"Damn." Bob shook his head. "There goes the government's case."

"Not really." John said. "I called his sponsoring attorney. He said they videotaped Anton's interviews and can use them at the trials." He looked at Paul. "You can shut down the protection detail and take the young lady back to her apartment."

"Why did Victor do it?" Bob asked.

"The dumb ass." John shook his head. "I guess he was more loyal to his family connections than he was the Marshals Service. The investigation is ongoing. I'm sure the FBI will come up with more information."

Paul walked to his desk and picked up three documents. He handed Bob a single page. "Earlier this morning she signed that voluntary termination. When she did, I told our guys to head home. Don't want to leave her at the hotel so I promised to drive her back to her apartment."

John shrugged. "Her decision. What's she going to do?"

"Leave town."

"Make sure she has our eight hundred number," Bob said. "She may need it."

"I will." He looked at John and then Bob. "There's one other thing I need to tell you." He handed both men a copy of a two page report.

They scanned the first page and looked at him.

"That's an up-to-date report from the surgeon that treated me when I got shot two years ago. Based on his findings, I'm submitting a request for a medical retirement."

"Why?" Bob asked.

"When you read his report you'll see that there's a good chance the bullet lodged near my spine could move. If it does, it might injure the spinal column. I'm not willing to take that chance."

John finished reading the doctor's report. "I can't say I blame you. Are you sure you want to do this?"

"Yes, I put a lot of thought into it."

"We're going to hate to lose you, but based on what the doctor said I understand your decision. When you have it ready, I'll hand-carry the paperwork to the right people at headquarters."

"Thanks, John."

Later that day Paul drove Tatiana to her apartment.

"Did you make arrangements for your furniture?" he asked.

"Yes. Wednesday. Everything will go in storage. I'll decide what I'm going to do with it later."

"The apartment management knows you're leaving?"

"Yes."

"And your diamonds?"

"I'm going to close my account and take them." She smiled. "Why did you say my diamonds? Don't you mean Anton's diamonds?"

This was his opportunity to tell her what had happened. "This morning I was told Anton was murdered in prison."

Her only reaction was a slight shrug. "He meant nothing to me. My relationship with him ended a long time ago."

She stepped in front of him, wrapped her arms around his waist. Their eyes met. "Thank you for being the nicest man I've ever met." She squeezed him and stepped back.

Paul smiled. "Thank you for being the best protected witness I've ever met."

CHAPTER XX

TIME TO DISAPPEAR

Less than a week later, Tatiana stood outside her apartment door.

The supervisor of the moving crew that had packed and loaded her furniture into his truck handed her a folder. "This is the inventory of everything we packed, Ms. Demko. The contract for storage, and a brochure from the company are in there."

She took the folder and handed him three twenty-dollar bills. "Thank you. The money is for you and the other two men."

"Thank you, ma'am. Where are you moving to?"

She smiled. "New York City."

"It's cold and expensive up there."

"I know, but it's my home. Have a good day." She walked into her vacant apartment and checked each room to make sure they had taken everything. On her way out the door, she grabbed her red carry-on bag and strolled to her car.

She placed the suitcase on the back seat, got in and lowered the convertible top.

As she drove past her apartment she slowed, glanced at the front door, and raised both arms "Today my old life ends, and my new life begins."

Five days after Tatiana had moved out, Paul walked to his office desk and took a seat. He picked up a single page handwritten by Tatiana.

A column listing what she had to do before she moved ran down the left side of the page.

He stared at the list and stopped on the final item. "Forwarding address, glad she didn't forget that."

He walked across the room and fed the page into the shredder.

Time to move on. Paul placed his set of keys in the center desk drawer and walked to the couch. As he picked up a cardboard box with his belongings in it, he turned a lingering look to his desk. *It was a great ride while it lasted.* He turned and walked out of his office.

An Uber driver pulled up in front of the building and he got in the back seat.

"Sneaking out of the office early?"

Paul chuckled. "I'm sneaking out for good. Just took an early retirement."

The driver looked at him in the mirror. "A little young to retire aren't you?"

"It doesn't matter what age you are. A man needs to do what makes him happy."

They did not speak again until the driver pulled into Paul's driveway.

Paul grabbed his box, got out of the car, and walked around to the driver's side. "Thank you for the lift."

The man stuck his hand out the window. "Good luck. Enjoy your retirement." He backed out of the driveway.

Paul walked to the front door and entered his condo. In the kitchen he set the box on a table, opened the refrigerator, and removed a bottle of beer. He twisted off the cap and took a long drink.

"You're home earlier than I thought."

He turned and held his arms out.

Tatiana wrapped her arms around him and planted a passionate kiss on his lips.

They held the embrace, and when he released her he grinned. "It was easier than I thought."

"When I'm ready all I need to do is call the company, and they'll ship the furniture wherever I want."

"Good. Can you think of anything else you need to do?"

"No."

"Then there's no reason to hang around any longer." He pulled two passports from his pocket and slid them on the counter. "You ready?"

She glanced at them. "I've been ready for a long time."

"Good. It looks as if everything worked out perfectly. Now it's time to disappear for a while."

THE END

www.ingramcontent.com/pod-product-compliance
Lightning Source LLC
Chambersburg PA
CBHW050123280326
41933CB00010B/1220